How to Get the Other 90% from your Amstrad PC 1512-1640

Martin Amor

THE DIVOX PRESS

The Divox Press
a division of Divox Limited

First published in the United Kingdom by the Divox Press 1987

Copyright © Martin Amor 1987

British Library Cataloguing in Publication Data

Amor, Martin
How to Get the Other 90% from your Amstrad PC 1512-1640
1. Amstrad PC1512-1640 (Computer)
I. Title
004.165   QA76.8.A4
ISBN 1-870473-00-0

This book was written on an Amstrad PC 1512 and was printed and bound in the United Kingdom. Further copies can be obtained by sending a cheque for £8.95 (postage and packing are free) made payable to Divox Limited, to the Divox Press, FREEPOST 1040, Gerrards Cross, Buckinghamshire, SL9 7BR.

Divox invites authors in all subject areas to submit manuscripts or proposals for future volumes and also welcomes suggestions and comments about this book. All correspondence should be sent to the Divox Press, P.O. Box 678, Gerrards Cross, Bucks., SL9 7UR.

Contents

Preface

All personal computer users, however experienced they may be, want to become more productive. First-time users are often amazed and deterred at how long it seems to take to get the PC to perform even the simplest task - after all that fiddling about, surely it would be faster to do it by hand? Experienced users, having fought and won those first battles, still have nagging doubts - is this really the quickest and easiest way to do it? Am I using more than 10% of my PC's potential?

This book aims to answer those questions and dispel those doubts by helping you to streamline your PC use. It will not provide a mass of technical detail with which to grapple in the small hours; it will give straightforward, practical advice to Amstrad PC 1512 and 1640 users at all levels. Both floppy and hard disk machines are catered for. The objectives are simple:

1 To save you time

2 To make Amstrad PC computing easier

3 To help you to stay out of trouble

There is a further goal. PC users who are fairly satisfied with their chosen application - accounting, financial planning, word process- ing, graphics or whatever - begin to ask: what else can my system do for me? This book includes detailed guidance on selecting software, as well as a brief survey of the packages available in each major area of application - and where to buy them. Most microcom- puters are obtained to do a single task; successful users are often surprised at the range of jobs they are tackling with their PCs in less than a year.

My thanks are due to all the software companies who were kind enough to let me review their products for Amstrad PC suitability. I should also like to thank Steven Mead for his helpful suggestions and my wife Janet for almost limitless tea and patience.

I wish you every success in getting the other 90% from your Amstrad PC!

Martin Amor

PART ONE
OVERVIEW

Chapter One
Boosting PC Performance

The ideas and advice in this book range from simple tips to fairly advanced techniques, so that all users should find some helpful material. Most of the ideas can be used independently, so you don't have to read the whole book before you can start to apply them, to make your PC work harder for you.

There are five simple ways of increasing your PC productivity; fortunately, the easiest methods often show the greatest returns.

I - Do Everyday Tasks the Quickest Way

Valuable time can be wasted by doing simple jobs in a complicated way, and even the easiest task can take much longer if you are not clear about what you are doing. Chapter 4 reviews all the essential skills for using your PC 1512 or 1640, with useful tips - and traps to avoid. Even experienced users may find some helpful advice.

II - Keep Out of Trouble

As many readers know to their cost, when things go wrong, the hours can disappear at an alarming rate. Just as you can learn 'defensive driving' in order to minimise potential accidents, Chapter 5 will help you to practise 'defensive computing' in order to avoid PC trouble. Some precautions will save far more time than they take, while some tempting 'shortcuts' can cost you dear in the long run.

If you do get into trouble, Chapter 6 will guide you back on course, while Chapter 7 concentrates on trouble-free printing.

III - Work Faster with GEM and DOS

Chapter 3 explains the relationship between your PC, GEM and MS-DOS (also DOS-Plus for 1512 users) throwing some light on which operating software you should be using when. Chapter 8 describes further time-saving techniques to streamline use of your PC. You will not learn about all the innermost intricacies of operating systems - but you will learn some powerful, practical ways of getting the best out of the operating software supplied with your Amstrad.

IV - Use the Right Software

Vital as GEM and DOS are, they are mere servants to the applications programs which actually do the job you want done. By the way, programs and software are interchangeable terms - and the applications software which you buy is often called packaged software, or just packages.

By using the right software in the right way you really harness the power of your PC. Chapter 9 will help you to choose good packaged software and Chapter 10 describes how to get it 'up and running'.

V - New Applications

When you feel that your PC is starting to earn its keep by making you more productive, you will probably ask: what next? In a book of this size it is impossible to analyse in detail the enormous range of possibilities open to the Amstrad user. A brief survey of some of the leading packages in the major application areas has, however, been included as an Appendix. Despite the brevity of these listings, most users will find at least one or two new ideas here. They might help you to decide on the next area to tackle - perhaps one which you hadn't considered before.

For those who are keen to develop their own systems (or hire someone to do it for them) some suggestions and, as usual, some warnings will be found in Chapter 9.

Symbols Used in This Book

 The warning triangle appears whenever you are strongly advised *not* to do something (or at least to proceed with great caution) - it is usually unwise, and might be very risky.

 The owl, on the other hand, indicates a strong recommendation: an action, safeguard or precaution which should prevent mistakes and/or reduce the risk of getting into trouble.

 The light bulb accompanies 'bright ideas'. Take them or leave them, these are not usually essential - but you may find them useful. They are intended to make Amstrad PC computing easier, faster and more enjoyable.

If you can't wait to take off the casing and get at your Amstrad PC with your soldering iron, this book is not for you. You will find (in the Appendix) brief details of a few of the major hardware 'add-ons' which you might consider, but before you rush off to dismantle your PC and bolt on new bits, bear in mind:

 Don't tinker with your hardware: modifications may invalidate your guarantee and your maintenance agreement - check with your dealer

Note: the Carriage Return ←⎯ and the Enter key on your PC keyboard are treated as interchangeable. Where a command in the text includes the word 'ENTER', pressing either key will work.

Chapter Two
The Amstrad PC 1512-1640

What makes the Amstrad PC such an excellent machine for the business, professional and home computer user? To answer that question we must look briefly at the eventful history of the PC.

Microcomputers appeared in the late 1970s: initially in the form of kits for electronics hobbyists, soon followed by the first true desktop computers. In a couple of years there was a bewildering range of micros available; serious computing was for the first time within the financial reach of millions of small businesses and individuals.

The trouble was that most manufacturers supplied hardware and software which was largely incompatible with everyone else's. Once you had a machine from one manufacturer you had to stay with them for both hardware and software: your programs would not run on anyone else's computers - and other suppliers' programs would not run on yours! This was often a deliberate policy, designed to 'lock customers in' to a particular company's products. Although first-time users were spoilt for choice in hardware, they could never be confident that their chosen manufacturer would survive - they often did not. Worse still, quality software was scarce.

The IBM PC, announced towards the end of 1981 (though not available in the UK until 1983), rapidly transformed the microcomputer industry. It was by no means a revolutionary machine, but IBM's sheer size and power ensured that their PC became the worldwide standard for microcomputers. A swarm of software companies homed in on the PC, assured of a huge potential market. Similarly, dozens of manufacturers developed IBM PC 'compatibles': machines which would do all that an IBM could - but would be cheaper and often more powerful.

Both these trends have greatly benefitted the PC user, who now enjoys a fantastic choice of 'off-the-shelf' software packages, along with reliable hardware at competitive prices.

This brings us back to the Amstrad PC, which is already one of the most successful computers ever. High-volume, low-cost production has enabled Amstrad to break previous price barriers - and a very high level of compatibility with the IBM standard gives the Amstrad buyer access to the largest possible range of software. Sales of the Amstrad PC 1512 and 1640 could well exceed a million.

Software companies, anxious to share this success, have launched low-cost versions of their programs to run on the Amstrad PC. They believe, understandably, that they are unlikely to sell these packages at their old prices, which would now be more than half the cost of the computer! So the Amstrad PC user can find superb software at very low prices.

Nobody should imagine that the Amstrad PC is a second-best computer for those who cannot afford the real thing. On the contrary, the Amstrad is neater and significantly faster than the original IBM PC. Its screen quality is higher, especially so with the enhanced graphics of the 1640, the user instruction book is good and the mouse is included in the price. For these and several other standard Amstrad features, the IBM user has to pay extra.

Chapter Three
Why All This Software?

Some PC buyers are lucky if they find a single floppy disk lurking in the polystyrene as they unpack their purchases; the Amstrad user receives four. (One more in fact for HD models and one less for 1640 users). But what are they all for?

Your colourful floppies mostly contain, as you know, operating software: programs which are no use at all in getting your invoices out, getting your (fictitious) heroine out of the desperate straits you wrote her into, getting your budgets done, and so on. For all those real jobs you need applications software. But you still cannot do without the operating software.

Even in a simple PC system, there is a lot happening. Data (numbers, words, instructions, etc.) is rushing in all directions: from the mouse and keyboard, to the screen, to and from the memory and the disks, perhaps to a printer. All this activity is on top of any actual calculation or other processing which may be taking place.

Operating Systems

An operating system is a 'traffic control' program, interpreting your instructions, receiving and transmitting data, sending out results to screen or disk or printer. Without it, you would have to organise and control all those flows of data around the system yourself. We can say, to keep things simple, that the main operating system for your Amstrad is MS-DOS.

MS-DOS is, fortunately, the worldwide standard operating system for PCs, which means that you can run virtually any PC software on your Amstrad, and MS-DOS will (in theory) take care of your input and output data and all the processing in between. PC-DOS, by the way, is simply a version of MS-DOS designed for the IBM PC: the two systems are more or less identical.

By typing in commands on the keyboard, you can use the operating system to carry out a range of useful, sometimes vital, tasks. So disk number 1 (the red one) contains all the programs and commands which together make up MS-DOS.

Despite being useful - even indispensable - MS-DOS is not the slightest bit 'friendly'. Like all operating systems, it was designed by a programmer for other programmers - and it shows. (The same goes, incidentally, for DOS-Plus). A lot of effort has therefore been put into designing an extra software 'layer' to make DOS more palatable; this sugar-coating is called GEM.

Of Mice and Menus - the purpose of GEM

With any system, it sometimes seems that you have too much information, too many options. PC users may have hundreds of files of data (text, numbers, pictures) stored on their systems - and a large assortment of programs and commands with which to mani-pulate it all. If a PC tries to display all those files or all those commands on the screen at once, it becomes extremely confusing. You may forget which file you want and type in the wrong com-mands by mistake. GEM, the software supplied on your Amstrad disks (numbers 2 and 3) provides simple ways of reducing this information overload.

Firstly, GEM displays only some of the programs and files stored on your system at any time: just the ones you want available for the moment. You view these files through a screen area called a GEM window, just as you can see into only one room of a house through a real window. When you want to shift your attention to another group of files, you simply open another window. The screen can be kept uncluttered by closing unwanted windows - they just disappear.

Secondly, GEM displays data files and programs in the form of pictures (icons) rather than text. This helps you to see more quickly, for example, which type of information is stored in each file, and to distinguish instantly between programs and data files.

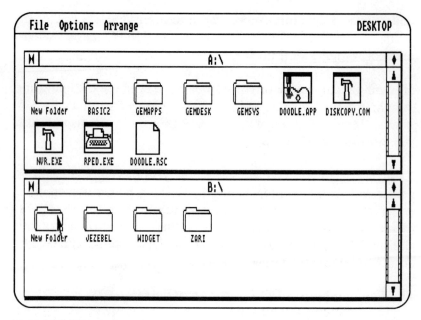

Typical GEM windows and icons

Thirdly, by using the mouse to move a pointer around the screen, GEM enables you to give instructions to your PC by pointing to icons or words on the screen - rather than typing in lengthy commands on the keyboard.

The actions and commands you require are often selected from menus which are 'pulled down' from the top of the screen: again, simply by pointing. When you have made your selection, the menu disappears again, otherwise the screen would become hopelessly cluttered.

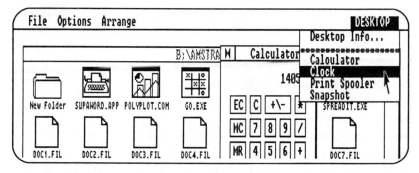

Making a selection from a GEM pull-down menu

Overall, GEM attempts to make working on your PC as straightforward and easy to understand as working at a desk: opening folders,
working on individual documents - even using a calculator and
checking the time! The difference should be that, with effective use
of good software, your productivity will be much higher with the
GEM 'Desktop'.

Why use DOS?

Given the benefits of GEM, you may feel that there is no reason to
bother with direct use of DOS itself. There are, however, a number
of important features of DOS which cannot be used from the GEM
Desktop. Furthermore, many powerful applications packages are
so hungry for storage that they will not happily co-exist with GEM.
As a general rule, it is suggested:

**Use MS-DOS when you need particular com-
mands or programs which are inaccessible from
GEM.**

The GEM software is spread across your blue and green master
floppy disks. But what about DOS-Plus, which (for PC 1512 users)
shares the yellow disk with the GEM Paint graphics program? This
operating system is an alternative to MS-DOS, with which it has
much in common.

MS-DOS or DOS-Plus?

The availability, on 1512 models, of both of these operating systems
is probably more confusing than helpful at first sight. Most users will
not want to spend valuable time learning a whole range of extra
commands when 99% of their computing can be handled by GEM
in conjunction with MS-DOS. But there might be, occasionally,
circumstances when DOS-Plus could be useful.

You might possibly want to run programs originally designed to run
under yet another operating system, CP/M-86, although in most
cases there will be an MS-DOS or PC-DOS version: use that
instead, if you have the choice. Some users will wish to switch

rapidly between English and other European languages, changing the way the keyboard behaves accordingly; DOS-Plus makes this easy.

With these occasional exceptions, however, the recommendation is:

If you are not using GEM, use MS-DOS. Don't spend valuable time learning DOS-Plus commands; there is a real danger of confusing them with similar-sounding MS-DOS commands, which can work in very different ways.

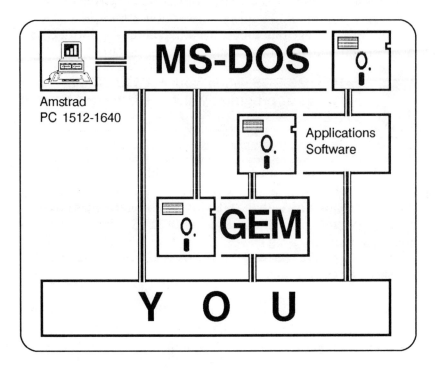

How you communicate, via your software, with your Amstrad PC

As you can see, operating systems are an essential link between you and your computer, but the more time you have to spend fiddling about with DOS (or GEM), the less time you have left for productive computing. Our goal must be to use operating software only as a tool to enhance, speed up, safeguard or streamline the real work of running your chosen application.

PART TWO
METHODS

Chapter Four
Simple Techniques for Easier Computing

In the next few pages we'll review the most essential skills needed to use your Amstrad PC. More experienced users may find that a recap will clarify a number of points, while first-time buyers should, definitely ensure that they are comfortable with everything in this chapter before trying any fancier techniques.

The Amstrad Manual

By now you have diligently studied, or at least glanced through, your Amstrad User Instructions book. This, believe it or not, is one of the best written and most clearly designed PC manuals around. You should not worry if some topics are still thoroughly confusing. Firstly, several of these subjects will become clear after a few weeks or months working with your machine. Secondly, there is far more information in there than most users will ever need to know: a wealth of detail about operating systems which less than one user in fifty really needs, and other technical information primarily aimed at programmers or designers.

Are you sitting comfortably?

Let's assume that, some time ago, you followed the instructions with care and succeeded in assembling your system. The next time you use it (try it now if your PC is available) make two simple checks which could be as valuable as two hundred 'hot tips'.

First, your posture: do you have to look down (or up) a long way to view the screen? Is it hard to reach the keyboard and mouse comfortably, keeping your wrists fairly close to the horizontal? Above all, do you find yourself having to slouch with your back rounded rather than arched? If you answer 'yes' to any of those questions, adjust your chair, your screen height or your keyboard until you are more comfortable. Second, the screen itself: is it at a comfortable viewing distance? Most people find two feet from eye to screen too far, one foot too close - but experiment to find your own optimum distance. It is equally important to adjust the brightness and contrast to the best combination. People tend to have their screens too bright; a rather dimmer screen is far less tiring.

You can of course spend large sums on designer workstations and 'seating concepts', but a cushion or similar expedient could save your bank account along with your back muscles. A screen filter is not so extravagant, especially if you are working in a brightly lit room. Try holding some polarising sunglasses up to your screen to see the effect.

Research has not, so far, proved any radiation hazards from working long hours at a PC - it has shown that back pain and eyestrain are quite common.

 Make sure you are physically comfortable when using your PC

The Four Media Storage Theory

Now all you have to do is get all your data into the PC, and sit back while it does the work. Of course you don't believe that, but where exactly should you store your data? My crude storage theory states that every scrap will be found in one of the four following places:

Computer's Memory (RAM)	always forgets - whenever you switch off, sometimes sooner
Your Memory	often forgets - can be at crucial moments
Computer's Disks	rarely forget - these lapses increase dramatically when you rely on their not occurring
Paper	never forgets - unless destroyed by fire

You must decide exactly how to distribute your vital data between these four media. Magnetic disks, such as your Amstrad floppies, are remarkably reliable, hard 'Winchester' disks even more so. They are so trouble-free that you begin to think that they are 100% reliable - and start counting on them. That's when they fail. Whether you are storing programs or data, words, numbers, pictures or whatever, the rule is the same:

 Always make at least one spare copy of all your computer files

You should certainly store spare copies of files on floppy disks, but for even greater peace of mind, don't rule out the humble sheet of paper. Ever since computer consultants started talking about 'the paperless office', paper has had, so to speak, a bad press. Most 'automated' offices are actually consuming paper as never before; the paperless office probably will arrive eventually but, for most of us, it is still some way off.

The point for the PC user is simple. If you have really vital information which you just cannot afford to lose - do not rely solely on your computer; print it out once in a while. How often depends on how often you create or change large amounts of information: monthly or weekly is enough for some people; others really need to make printouts daily. Even the careful user who takes several 'backup' copies of disks will sleep better with an old-fashioned printout in the cupboard.

 For irreplaceable files, make an extra copy on paper

I make no apology for stressing this need for 'backup' copies of all your files; indeed we'll be returning to backups, and how to streamline them, later in the book. More PC users' time is probably wasted by 'lost data' than by any other single problem.

Your Filing System

If you are using a hard disk, you can draw a fairly accurate parallel between the disk and a single drawer of a filing cabinet. Both devices allow you to store a number of folders, each of which can contain a number of documents or smaller folders (or a mixture of the two).

A floppy disk is perhaps better compared to a large folder, which might have room for smaller folders: you could use such a folder for household bills, say, with separate, smaller, folders for electricity, gas, telephone, etc. Similarly, your floppy disk might contain individual folders for personal letters and business letters.

But with only 360 kilobytes (about 360,000 characters) of space available on a floppy disk (much less if you allow space for altering existing documents and a safety zone) there is little point in having a complicated structure with many folders within folders. To give you a rough guide, about 100 A4 word-processed pages is plenty to store on a single floppy disk. So if you are using floppies as your main storage method, keep it simple. Use plenty of disks, and keep related documents together on a disk of their own.

A document, by the way, is GEM's catch-all term for almost anything you might want to store on disk. It could be a memo, letter, report, spreadsheet data, forecast, orders file, payroll file, stock file, customer names and addresses list, graph, drawing, price list... as far as GEM is concerned, they are all documents. The icons (pictorial symbols) GEM uses to represent documents resemble a sheet of paper; you can get the sheet decorated with another symbol to show at a glance the different types of document you have stored - see Chapter 10).

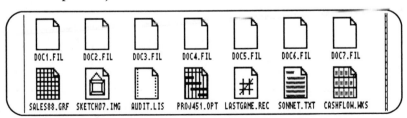

GEM document icons. The symbols on the second row help you to tell quickly what type of information each document contains.

As well as various documents, you will need to store programs on your disks, whether applications programs (e.g. word processing, accounting, spreadsheet, graphics, etc.) or so-called utility programs, many of which are provided with the operating system (e.g. programs for copying, comparing, editing, sorting, etc.). In either case, GEM represents programs by rectangular icons with solid bars along the top. The icons can also be enhanced with symbols intended to show what type of program you are dealing with.

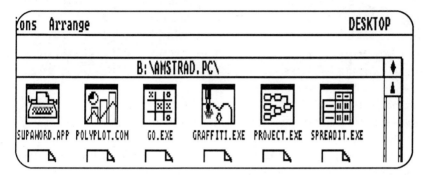

GEM program icons

Now DOS (by which I mean either MS-DOS or DOS-PLUS) isn't helpful enough to show you icons, and calls every item you have stored on disk a file, whether it is a letter, a list of names and addresses, a payroll program, a program to make copies of disks, or a program to humiliate you at chess.

Note also that a directory is just another name for a folder, i.e. a group of documents and/or programs. When you look at the contents of a GEM folder, you therefore find exactly the same items as in the DOS directory of the same name. The main directory of a particular disk, which shows all the folders (subsidiary directories) and files (documents or programs) stored there, is called the *root* directory.

Item	What GEM calls it	What DOS calls it	Examples
A list or display of everything on a disk	Root Directory	Root Directory	Shown by A:\, B:\ or C:\
A list or display of a particular group of files on a disk	Folder, shown by folder icon	(Sub-) Directory	B:\LETTERS\, A:\GEMSYS\
A list or display of a particular group of files within another group of files	Folder, shown by folder icon	(Sub-) Directory	B:\LETTERS\FIN\, C:\ACCTS\JOOST\
An individual document such as a letter	Document, shown by document icon	File	BANK0188.TXT, STANDLET
A set of data e.g. for a financial forecast	Document, shown by document icon	File	SREV8889.DAT, QTR3DEBT.CAL, PLANB.WKS
A program e.g. to help you to make a forecast or to play chess	Program, shown by program icon	File	MEGACALC.EXE, CHESS27.COM
A utility program e.g. one that you can use to copy disks	Program, shown by program icon	File	DISKCOPY.COM, DISKCOPY.EXE, DISK.CMD

A Guide to MS-DOS and GEM Terminology

The figure should help to clarify the confusing terms used by GEM and MS-DOS to describe items stored on your Amstrad PC.

File Names

Any document or program is identified by its two-part name, which you can choose or alter to suit your needs. The first part is the filename itself, which can be up to eight characters long. You can leave it at that, but often filenames have an extension, which can be up to three characters long, called the filetype. Typical examples of complete names are COMMAND.COM, REPORT07.DOC, ZARI, QBASIC.EXE, AUTOEXEC.BAT, JEZEBEL (all these are acceptable names).

 Don't forget to put the full stop between the file-name and any filetype there may be, or else your file cannot be found.

Don't put spaces in your filenames; MY FILE will be stored as MY, if at all; searching for MYFILE will draw a blank.

Certain types of file *must* include the filetype as part of the name:

Programs set up to run with GEM must be of filetype .APP, e.g. DOODLE.APP on your GEM Desktop disk.

Programs which you can run directly from MS-DOS must have filetype .COM or .EXE, e.g. SF4.COM, MAGIWORD.EXE.

Programs which you can run directly from DOS-Plus must have filetype .COM, .CMD or .EXE e.g. SF4.COM, PURCH.CMD.

BASIC programs must be contained in files of filetype .BAS e.g. DEMO.BAS, WORDGAME.BAS.

Many applications programs let you create files for your data with a filename of your choice, to which they automatically tack on an appropriate filetype. So a best-selling database package stores your data in .DBF files, a spreadsheet program uses .WKS (worksheet) files, a word processing program uses .DOC files and GEM Paint (supplied with your PC) stores your masterpieces as .IMG files.

Meaningful Names

It is a useful habit to take a moment to think up a sensible name each time you create a new document. In a week's time you will almost certainly have forgotten what FRED or ADA actually contain. LETTER would be an improvement, but not much if you are intending to store more than one letter on disk. If so, why not have one disk entirely for letters, and use, for example, names like BANK0188, AMS0288, to indicate the addressee and date. Work out your own system, but your objective should be to use filenames which will give you a good idea, even after a year or so, as to the file's contents.

 Careful choice of filenames will help to organise your data and save you hours of frustrating searching for lost information

Stick to using letters and numbers only when making up your filenames: it keeps life simpler. The same rules on forming names apply to folders (directories); it is equally important to choose sensible names for them.

STARTING UP

There are several ways of starting a program running on your Amstrad PC, depending on your machine, the type of program, how it has been set up to run and whether you are just starting or in the middle of a computing session. Whenever you run a program, make sure that you are using a working copy, not the original master program. Copying disks and files is reviewed later in this chapter.

 Never use master copies of programs; use backup copies, having carefully stored the originals

Hard disk users should have copied their software onto their hard disk, both for security and speed and convenience in operation. Any data files: word processed documents, numerical data, screen images or whatever, will probably also be stored on the hard disk (we'll see later how to keep data and programs separate on a hard disk).

If you are running your programs from floppies, however, you must still decide where to store your data files. Some people cram these files on the same disk as their applications programs. This is not recommended; even if you have room, there is always a slight danger of corrupting or overwriting your actual program.

If using floppies, keep all data files on separate disks from your applications programs.

This is an important exception to the general guideline which floppy disk users rapidly discover: keep floppy switching to a minimum! One way of achieving this is to set up the program so that it automatically loads and runs from a floppy disk, with no need to key in commands first. These so-called turnkey programs are quite easy to set up, as we shall see in Chapters 8 and 10, and can save quite a lot of time. The same method can equally be used to run a program automatically from a hard disk.

Running programs from floppy disks: SD and DD machines

Whatever type of program you want to use, and however it has been set up to run, using the flowchart overleaf should show you the basic steps to follow in order to get it working. On dual-drive 'DD' PCs, the left-hand floppy drive is drive A, the right-hand drive is drive B. If you are using a single-drive 'SD' PC, your disk drive can be called either drive A or drive B. Sometimes a program will ask you to insert a disk into drive A, sometimes into drive B! This can be confusing; just try to remember which disk you have in your machine at any particular moment.

Changing to a different program

If you want to switch during a computing session to using a different program, the following procedure is suggested:

1) Exit from the previous program in the correct way.
2) If the new program is set up to run in the same way as the previous one (e.g. from GEM), ensure that you are in the correct folder (directory) for the new program.

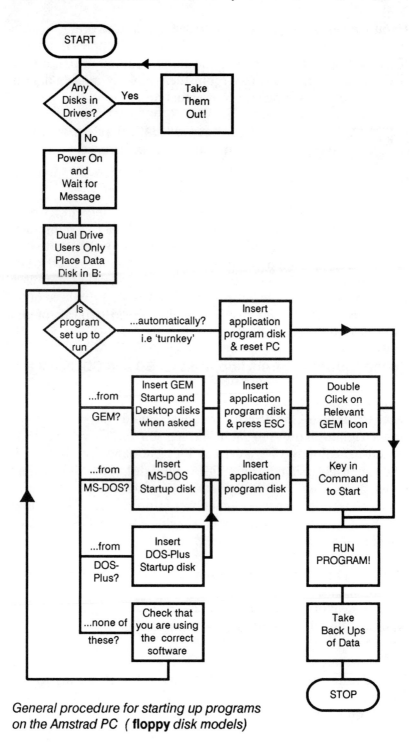

*General procedure for starting up programs on the Amstrad PC (**floppy** disk models)*

3) If the new program is set up to run in a different way e.g. runs from MS-DOS whereas the previous program was a GEM package, insert the appropriate start-up disk e.g. MS-DOS start-up. Reset your system by holding down the Alt and Ctrl keys while you press the Del key. This is called a 'warmstart'.

4) Enter the command to start the new program.

 Never 'warmstart' (i.e. reset with Ctrl, Alt, Del) your PC if you have anything stored in your PC's main memory (RAM) which you have not yet saved on disk

Running programs from hard disk: HD or upgraded machines

With the luxury of a hard disk, you should hardly ever need to use your GEM or DOS 'startup' disks. You should have followed the Hard Disk Installation Instructions to copy all this operating software from floppy to hard disk. Your applications software should also be copied onto the hard disk and installed/configured for ease of use (see Chapter 10). Indeed, you will probably have only two normal uses for floppy disks:

1) loading up new software
2) making backup copies of data (or new programs)

The procedure for switching to run a different program during a session is the same as that given above for floppy disk machines, except that, in step 3, you will not need to insert a 'startup' floppy disk - all the startup software for GEM or DOS should be on your hard disk.

The flowchart overleaf takes hard disk users through the startup procedure for running all kinds of software. If you have a hard disk in your PC, you can definitely save time (especially if you use several different programs) by using batch files to issue commands automatically (see Chapters 8 and 10).

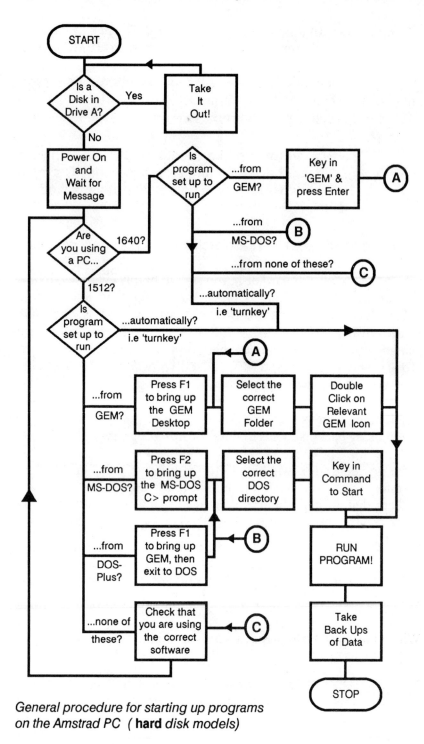

*General procedure for starting up programs
on the Amstrad PC (**hard** disk models)*

PREPARING YOUR DISKS

Before you can use any floppy disk, whether for storing your data files or for making working copies of your programs, it must be formatted. This process organises the space on a disk into neat zones ready for storing data; it is roughly analogous to ruling lines or a grid on a blank sheet of paper, before anything is written on it.

If you have a single disk system, exit to DOS (ensuring that your MS-DOS disk is in the disk drive) and type FORMAT ENTER. You will then be prompted to place the disk to be formatted into the disk drive. Place your blank disk in the disk drive and press any key to start the formatting process.

With a dual-floppy system, close all windows until you have just the window with the disk drive icons displayed, as shown:

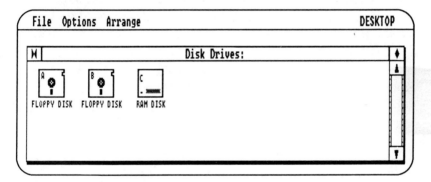

GEM window showing disk icons

Insert your blank disk in drive B, and click once on the drive B icon. Then pull down the File menu, and select the Format option. If you are certain that the disk is empty, or that you want to obliterate any files on it, click on OK in the Dialog box. Otherwise, you still have a chance to click on Cancel.

With a hard disk system, the process is similar, except that drive A is the one to format. Whatever you do, remember:

 Do not format drive C, unless you want to wipe every single file from your hard disk.

Give some thought to how you want to organise your files on disk, and label any floppy disks accordingly. Write the date and details of files on the label before you stick it on the disk - without pressing too hard. Sometimes you may feel you have to write on a label when it is already on the disk; if you must, use a soft fibre-tipped pen and write very gently.

Formatting disks is a nuisance. To minimise the time spent:

 Format each box of disks all at once when you buy them. Better still, if you value your time, buy them pre-formatted. Ten floppy disks take 15 to 20 minutes to format.

RAMDISKS

If you are using a single- or dual-floppy disk machine, you will have noticed the drive C 'RAM DISK' icon displayed on your GEM Desktop. This is an area of your PC's main memory (RAM) which has been set aside to store files as if it were an extra disk drive. When you start up GEM your PC automatically sets up a RAM disk of 34K (about 34,000 characters) on to which it copies some system files, thus making a number of basic DOS commands available without any disk swapping.

A RAM disk can be useful because reading and writing data to and from RAM is much faster than using real (floppy) disks. If you can work with your data file(s) in RAM, storing or amending them appears to be almost instantaneous. This speed is invaluable if you are dealing with lengthy documents or large data files. A RAM Disk is almost essential if your PC has only a single floppy disk drive.

There are, however, two drawbacks. First, if you are running GEM on a PC 1512 without upgraded memory you will not have room for a RAM Disk larger than 34K: not enough to be really useful. Second, if you do use a RAM disk for high-speed storage and manipulation of files, you must remember to copy them to a real disk before switching off or resetting the computer. Your applications program may remind you to do this, but some programs do not - you just have to remember.

Files stored on a RAM Disk are lost when your PC is switched off

We shall explore the practical use of RAM Disks in Chapter 8.

EXAMINING YOUR DISKS

When you open a GEM window on a disk (by double-clicking on the disk icon for the drive you want to look at) your GEM desktop displays an icon for each of the files stored in the root directory of that disk. Notice that the title of the window shown below is B:\, indicating that it is the root directory of drive B. If there are shaded areas visible on the vertical scroll bar, you know that there are more files on that directory than you can currently see in the window. Click on the diamond-shaped full box (at the top right hand corner of the window) to expand the window to full screen size. If there are still more files, click on the up and down arrows to scroll the window up and down.

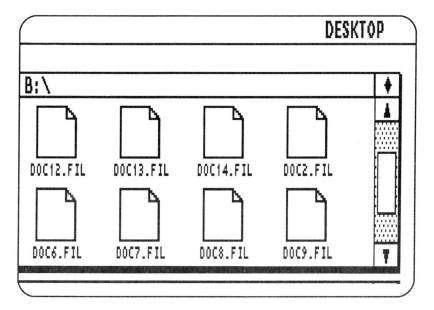

GEM window with scroll bar indicating that there are more files than the window is currently showing.

The icons, together with their filenames, will tell you what type of documents and programs you have stored on disk. It is often useful to know the size of each file and when it was created. By pulling down the Arrange menu and clicking on the Show as Text option, these details are displayed. The date, by the way, may not be the date the file was first created; it is the creation date or the date of the last change or amendment, whichever is the later. Repeat the same process to show your files as icons again. Selecting the other options on this menu allows you to rearrange the display: in alphabetical order, or in order of size or date - even in order of file type.

```
  File  Options  Arrange                                      DESKTOP

  ▶|                              A:\                           |◆
     ◆ New Folder          00-00-80  00:00                      ▲
     ◆ BASIC2              09-07-86  13:54
     ◆ GEMAPPS             09-07-86  13:54
     ◆ GEMDESK             09-07-86  13:54
     ◆ GEMSYS              09-07-86  13:55
       DOODLE    APP  28672 01-01-80  03:23
       DISKCOPY  COM   8832 20-06-86  16:57
       NUR       EXE   8596 04-07-86  09:28      ▶
       RPED      EXE   4612 14-07-86  15:37
       DOODLE    RSC   2388 09-07-86  10:37




                                                               ▼
```

Files shown in text form by GEM

To examine another disk, simply double-click on that disk's icon; if you can't see it, close windows (by clicking on the close box at the top left of any window) until the disk icons are revealed. If you are actually inserting a different disk, you must tell your PC by pressing ESC.

 Remember to press ESC (or double-click on the relevant disk icon) when you change disks, or your screen may show files which are no longer there.

To examine another folder, double-click on the folder's icon to open a window on that folder. Notice how the title at the top of the window shows the name of that particular folder e.g. A:\LETTERS\. When you examine a folder within another folder, the name at the top of the window extends, showing the new directory and, in effect, how you can get there e.g. A:\LETTERS\FINANCE\ i.e. find drive A, open folder LETTERS, and from there open folder FINANCE.

Examining disks with DOS

If you are using DOS directly, rather than GEM, the same file information is obtained by the DIR command. At the DOS prompt (A>, B> or C>) type DIR ENTER. The root directory of the default drive (i.e. the drive which DOS is currently working with) is displayed. If you have more than a 'screenful' of files, you can compress the display by typing DIR/W ENTER, which will show your files across the screen. However, you will lose the date and size information; typing DIR/P ENTER instead will give you all the details, but only one page or screenful at a time.

To view files on another disk with DOS, simply specify the drive you want e.g. DIR C: ENTER (or DIR C:/P ENTER). This will show all files on the root directory of drive C (whether this is a RAM disk or a hard disk). If you are actually inserting a different floppy disk, there is no harm in checking its directory in any case, just to make sure it contains what you think it does!

 Don't forget the colon when specifying the drive. If you type DIR C ENTER, the system will reply 'File not found' - unless you happen to have a file called C on your default drive.

The default drive

One disk drive always has priority as the main drive on which you are working; this 'default' drive is where DOS will look for your existing files, and store your new files - unless you tell it otherwise. You can change the default drive in DOS by simply keying in e.g. A: (or B: or C:) ENTER. The DOS prompt will change to show the new default drive e.g. C>.

The default directory

Just as the drive with which your PC is currently working is called the default drive, so the current directory is called the default directory; much of the time, this will be the root (i.e. main) directory. The default directory is just as easy to change: in GEM, as we have seen, you just double-click on the appropriate folder icon in order to open a window on that folder. The DOS equivalent of opening a window to examine another folder is the Change Directory CHDIR (or CD) command. The format is:

CHDIR [drive:] [\] path

For example, typing CD C:\WORDPROC ENTER takes you into the directory called WORDPROC on drive C, whereas typing in CD A:\BASIC2\PROGRAMS\EXAMPLES ENTER takes you into the EXAMPLES directory within the PROGRAMS directory within the BASIC2 directory on drive A. The DIR command will then list only those files within the EXAMPLES directory.

To go back to the root directory in DOS (equivalent to closing folders in GEM until just the A:\ (or B:\ or C:\) window is open, you simply type CD A:\ (or CD B:\ or CD C:\) ENTER.

Where am I?

It is quite easy to get lost in DOS, or to 'lose' files because you have forgotten which directory you are in. DOS does not always tell you where you are, unlike GEM with its helpful name above each folder's window. This can be easily remedied by issuing a PROMPT command. This can take several forms, but perhaps the most useful is to type PROMPT pg ENTER. This will replace the normal DOS prompt (A > etc.) with a prompt showing you the default drive and the current directory. We'll see later how to issue this and other DOS commands automatically whenever you start up your system.

Use the PROMPT pg command to keep track of which directory you are using

Finding files

You can look for individual files on disk by specifying the name, e.g.
DIR A:BUDGET88.WKS will list only that file, if it can be found
in the current directory. If you know the file should be in another
directory, called BUDGETS, for example, you can specify this in
the DIR command e.g. DIR B:\BUDGETS\BUDGET88.WKS
will list the details of the BUDGET88 worksheet file, even though
it is not in the default directory.

Wildcards

Files of similar name or type can be located by using wildcards. For
example, DIR *.WKS will list all files of filetype .WKS in the current
directory. An * represents any number of valid characters in the
relevant part of a name. So DIR REPORT.* would cause all files
named REPORT to be listed, irrespective of filetype.
REPORT.DOC, REPORT.BAK, REPORT, REPORT.ABC
would all appear. (In fact DIR REPORT will do the same.)
Conversely, DIR *.IMG will list all files of filetype .IMG, no matter
what they are called.

The ? character can be used as a wildcard to represent any single
valid character. So DIR ACC?????.* would list, for example,
ACCOUNTS.DBF,   ACC01234.CAL,   ACCTSMAP,
ACCCHART.999, but would not show ACC01.CAL because the
filename contains too few characters.

You may have noticed that DOS directories list files without the full
stop between filename and filetype. However, you must remember
to:

 **Include the full stop between name and type when
typing file and directory names - or else DOS will
not find the file(s) you are looking for.**

Some PC users find that their DOS directories insist on displaying
the dates in American format (MMDDYY). Some programs leave
it up to you to tell your computer that you want dates in UK format
(DDMMYY), which is achieved by a simple change to a file called
CONFIG.SYS. This process is described in Chapter 8.

COPYING FILES (programs or documents)

The ability to copy files is crucial to safe and trouble-free PC computing. All users spend quite a lot of time making copies of programs and data files, mostly for security reasons. Later on, we shall explore some ways of speeding up and automating this process; for the moment, let us examine the basic techniques.

GEM makes copying files extremely simple. First make sure that the icon for the file you want to copy - the 'source' file - is visible in one Desktop window, and that there is also a window open for the disk/folder where you want to store the copied file - the 'destination' folder. The destination must be on a disk which has been formatted; it doesn't matter if there are other files already on this disk, as long as there is enough free space. Free space on a disk is shown, in GEM, by clicking on the disk icon, then on the Info/Rename option of the GEM File Menu (in DOS, use the DIR command).

Use the mouse to point to the icon of the source file, then hold down the lefthand mouse button, keeping it held down until you have moved the pointer (which should have changed into a hand symbol) to an empty space in the window of the destination folder.

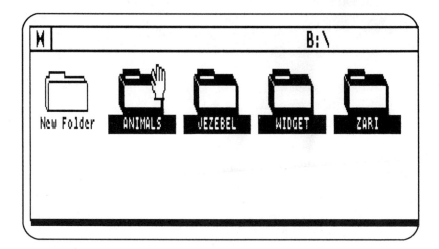

The GEM hand symbol during copying

Now release the mouse button, and the Copy Folders/Items Dialog box will appear. If you are copying just one item, the box will look like this:

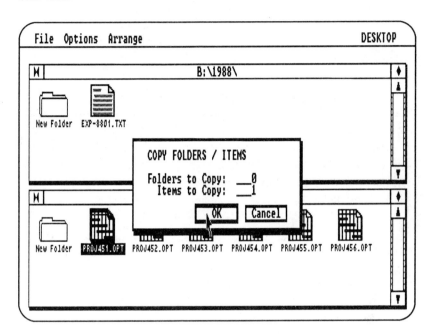

The Copy Folders/Items Dialog Box

If you are sure you want to go ahead with the copy, move the pointer to OK in the dialog box and click the lefthand mouse button once more. GEM will now copy the file as you have requested.

You can copy a whole folder, and thus all the files within it, (or even an entire disk) in exactly the same way: you simply click on a folder (or disk) icon instead of a single file, and follow the same procedure.

To copy several files within a folder, hold down the righthand mouse button and move the pointer to each icon in turn, clicking the lefthand mouse button before moving to the next icon. This will highlight as many icons as you want to copy; with the pointer over one of them, now hold down the lefthand mouse button, and move the pointer as before to an empty space in the destination folder.

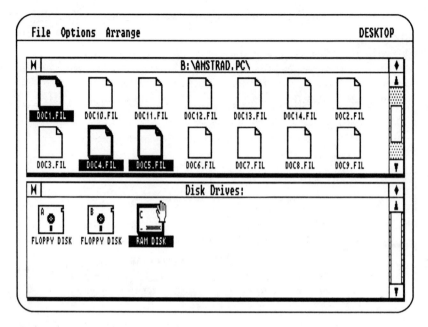

Copying several items at once with GEM

All the selected files/folders will now be copied, after you have selected OK in the Dialog Box.

GEM will tell you if there is insufficient space to complete your copying operation, in which case you must do some 'housekeeping' to clear some disk space before trying the copy again. It will also warn you if there is a 'name conflict', which arises if, say, you are trying to copy a file to a folder which already contains a file of the same name. A Name Conflict Dialog Box appears:

The Name Conflict Dialog Box

In such cases, you must choose from four options:

1) type in a new name for the copy to avoid any conflict.
2) replace the existing file by the new (copied) file by selecting the OK exit button.
3) omit to copy this particular file by selecting Cancel. GEM will then copy any other file(s) you may have selected.
4) abandon the whole copy operation by selecting Stop.

Copying with DOS

DOS makes you work a little harder to copy files, as you normally have to type in the relevant file name(s) when using the COPY command. There are three COPY formats for copying disk files:

1) COPY C:STK3456 A: copies the file called STK3456 from drive C to drive A (NOT the other way round). A path can be specified e.g. COPY C:\LETTERS\AMS0188.LET A:\MKTG copies the file called AMS0188.LET in the directory called LETTERS on drive C into the directory called MKTG on drive A. The copied file is still called AMS0188.LET.

2) COPY C:CURRENT.DAT A:PERIOD07.DAT copies CURRENT.DAT from drive C to drive A, changing the name (of the copy only) to PERIOD07.DAT. Again, paths can be specified.

3) COPY A:YREND87 simply copies YREND87 from drive A, placing the copy in the current directory of the default drive. If the root directory of A was the default directory in this case, an error message would occur, as a file cannot be copied to itself.

DOS does not, however, protect you from name conflicts; if the destination directory has a file of the same name already on it, DOS will simply overwrite it with the copy. This is fine if you wanted, say, to replace an old version of a file with a newer version - but not if you wanted to keep both.

 Take care not to wipe out data which you need by the incorrect use of COPY

One further copying hazard:

 If you attempt to replace an old file with a more recent version by COPYing and there is not enough room on disk, the old version may be erased, leaving neither version on the destination disk.

Wildcards and copying

Wildcards allow useful short cuts when copying with DOS. For example, COPY C:*.LET A: will copy all files with extension LET from drive C to drive A (as long as there is enough room on A - if not, the copying operation will not be completed).

Similarly, COPY A:\PARTS*.* B: will copy every file in the PARTS directory on drive A to the default directory on drive B.

Copying disks in one operation

As you can see, wildcards could be used to copy all the files on a disk in one operation (e.g. COPY A:*.* B:). However, to be sure of getting an exact, identical copy of a whole disk, use the MS-DOS DISKCOPY command. If you have a single-drive system, this is the easiest way of copying disks. Make sure that the DISKCOPY.EXE file is available (it is supplied on floppy disk No. 1), preferably on the default drive (if you have two).

Type DISKCOPY A: B: ENTER and the system will ask you to:

Insert source diskette in drive A
Insert target diskette in drive B

Press any key when ready

 Take care not to touch a key accidentally - or move the mouse - until you are ready to start the DISKCOPY process. If you do, your PC will start copying whichever disks you happen to have loaded, possibly wiping out vital data.

Copying disks on a single drive system

Keying in DISKCOPY A: A: ENTER will enable you to copy a floppy disk on a single drive PC. MS-DOS will prompt you to place the source diskette and the target diskette alternately in drive A. If you forget which is which, you're in trouble.

 Label your disks before starting any copying operation, so that you will never confuse your original (source) disk and your copy (target) disk.

A useful feature of DISKCOPY is that the target disk need not be formatted in advance; DISKCOPY will check whether the target disk is not yet formatted and, if required, will announce that it is:

Formatting while copying

If the target disk is already formatted, however, DISKCOPY will *not* stop to ask you whether it contains any vital files: they will just be obliterated.

You can perform a DISKCOPY from GEM, by double-clicking on the DISKCOPY.COM icon on the GEM Desktop, then entering parameters to indicate which disk you want to copy, e.g. A: B: (Incidentally, this procedure uses a special DISKCOPY utility program rather than the DOS command itself; the results are the same.)

Renaming Files and Folders

There are several reasons why you might want to rename a file or a folder, for example:

The original name was misspelt.

The original name had an incorrect filetype (extension). (e.g. BASIC-2 programs must have an extension BAS, or they cannot be run).

To distinguish clearly two similar files, or a 'live' file from a 'backup' file.

To rename under GEM, click once on the relevant icon, then pull down the File Menu (top left) and select the Info/Rename option. The cursor changes from the usual pointer into a vertical bar in the Item Info/Rename Dialog Box.

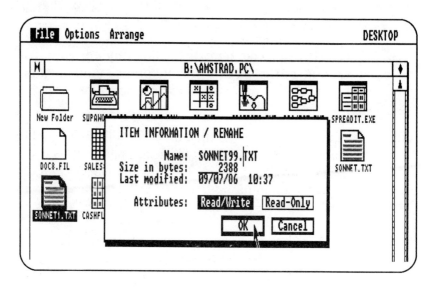

The Info/Rename Dialog Box

Press ESC to clear the existing name and type in the new name. Click on OK to complete the renaming process, which can be carried out on files or folders.

Renaming under DOS is also easy. The command format is:

REN old-file-details new-name ENTER

Old-file-details can be just the name, such as YREND88.BAK (the system will look for this file on the default drive and directory) or can include a drive and/or path, such as B:\SALES\PLAN8889.WKS. Examples:

REN YREND88.BAK FINAL88.DOC ENTER
REN C:\CO\LETTERS\FRED.LET ADA.LET ENTER

Simple Techniques for Easier Computing **41**

Deleting Files and Folders

Deleting files is dangerously simple. From the GEM Desktop you simply click the lefthand mouse button once over the icon(s) of the file(s) or folder(s) you want to delete, so as to highlight them. (You can delete any number in a single operation as long as they are all within a single folder.) Then pull down the File menu and select Delete. A dialog box appears:

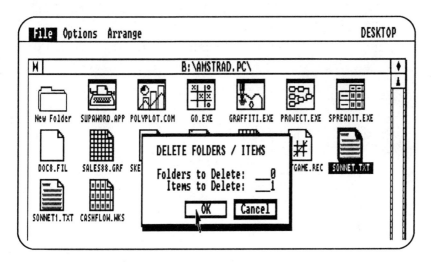

The Delete Folders/Items Dialog Box

If you are sure about your deletion(s), click on OK, otherwise you can still Cancel and think again.

To delete a file in DOS, the command format is:

DEL file-details ENTER

The DEL does not signify one of the 'Del' keys on your keyboard, but the letters D, E and L. File-details can be just a filename, or can include a drive and/or directory specification (as with RENaming above). Note that wildcards can be used - with devastating effect - with the DEL command. DEL *.DOC, for example, will delete all files of extension DOC in the default directory - without delay.

You cannot use DEL to delete a directory itself, only the files it contains. DEL *.* will delete every single file in the directory, although in this case DOS does give you one last chance to recant by asking:

Are you sure (Y/N)?

Which files on which disk?

As mentioned earlier, it is a good idea to keep your actual programs well apart from your data files. So if you are using floppies, keep a separate data disk for each application (or several of course, if you are storing large volumes of information).

If you are a hard disk user, set up a separate folder for each application, otherwise your Desktop/directory will become very cluttered. In GEM, just double-click on the New Folder icon, name the folder in the dialog box and click on OK.

To create a new directory (the DOS name for a folder) in DOS, using the MKDIR (or MD) command, type in:

MKDIR [drive:] [\] directory-pathname ENTER

For example MKDIR \LETTERS ENTER will set up a directory called LETTERS within the root directory of the default drive, while MKDIR C:\CO\ACCOUNTS will set up a directory called ACCOUNTS within the CO directory on drive C.

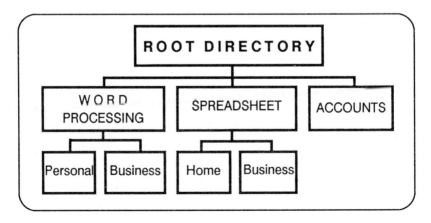

A typical Hierarchical Directory Structure

The rules for making up directory/folder names are similar to those for filenames. Keep to the alphabet and the digits 0-9 to make up simple, meaningful names.

 The DOS MKDIR (MD) command only creates a new directory; it does not change the current directory.

To change directories in DOS, use the CHDIR (or CD) command e.g:

CHDIR\C:\GROUP\ACCOUNTS ENTER

To go back the the root directory of the default drive, type:

CHDIR\ ENTER

A directory can be removed in DOS only by the RMDIR (or RD) command. The directory must be completely empty, so delete all files in it before trying the RMDIR command. The format is similar to MKDIR:

RMDIR [drive:] [\] directory-pathname ENTER

 Don't make your directory structure too complex: it is recommended that you never have more than three levels.

FINISHING A SESSION

Whenever you have finished a job on your PC, keep in mind two simple, but essential, points. Firstly, are all the files you have been working with, whether creating or amending, completely safe and secure from loss? Secondly, always be sure to exit from your programs in the correct way: *never* just switch off! We will discuss the problems caused by an over-hasty exit from an applications program in the next chapter, as we examine the most common causes of disaster for the PC user - and how they can all be avoided.

Chapter Five
Avoiding Disasters - The Top Twenty Traps

Problems great and small

When using a PC, or any other tool, problems are bound to occur. The vast majority of them will be minor and easy to solve. These include, for example, mistakes in entering commands (which cause an error message and are simply corrected), trying to run programs from the wrong operating system, wrong directory or wrong disk (usually harmless), misaligned paper (abandon printing and try again), and so on. Many such problems are dealt with in this book; Appendix VII of the Amstrad manual lists system error messages and should help you out of quite a few minor difficulties.

Other problems are on a different scale. The term 'disaster' here should be understood to mean not just fire, flood, etc. (although you should plan to mitigate the effects of these) but anything which will cost a significant amount of your time. Nearly always, this type of problem involves loss or corruption of data.

Defensive Computing

The next chapter provides a number of ideas which may help you out of trouble *after* the event - but sometimes nothing can retrieve your data: the only course is the painful one of reconstructing it piece by piece. The hackneyed proverb. 'prevention is better than cure' is doubly true for the PC user. Most disasters can be avoided: 'defensive computing' is about ensuring that they are very rare events indeed - and limiting the damage when they do occur.

I have identified twenty of the most common causes of PC disaster. The criteria for inclusion were simple: I have encountered each one of them at least twice, and on each occasion the problem had caused the user considerable grief. Some of them can crop up for a variety of reasons. They are not mutually exclusive, however; a single oversight could result in any one of several possible mishaps.

These are all problems which can afflict experienced users as well as first-timers; indeed, I have been on the receiving end of a few of them myself! This chapter is about serious trouble - and how to avoid it.

DISASTER CAUSE NUMBER 1 : Starting Up

What can go wrong with the simple process of starting up your PC? Perhaps the most common mistake is that of trying to insert a disk when the disk drive is just starting up; this can ruin the disk and, in the worst cases, damage the disk drive itself. When you switch on a floppy disk PC, the safest method is to *wait*.... until the system asks you to insert a system disk and the green light has definitely gone out over the disk drive(s). Then insert whichever startup disk you want to use (GEM, MS-DOS, DOS-PLUS or any other, customised, startup disk).

You do in fact have several seconds between the moment you switch on and the moment the system tries to read the disk drive(s); you can insert your startup disk then, but you run the risk described above. It probably is not worth the few seconds saved. Hard disk users will not face this problem, as they will generally start up their systems without a floppy disk. Hard disk users may occasionally need to start up from a floppy, in order to use a program which is not permanently installed on the hard disk. Even then it is probably worth waiting for the system to 'boot' (i.e. start up) from the hard disk, wait for the red (hard disk) light to go out, *then* insert the floppy into drive A and reset the PC (Ctrl, Alt, Del).

You certainly will not save time in the long run by leaving your startup disk (or any other disk) in the drive when the machine is switched off. Whenever you switch the PC on (or off) make sure that there are no floppy disks in the drive(s) - see the flowcharts on pages 24 and 26. Never use the mains switch on the wall socket to switch your PC on or off; it could possibly cause a damaging power surge through your equipment. Always switch on (and off) with the power switch at the back of your PC monitor, having first checked that the mains plug is firmly in the socket with the power on. If the fuse has blown in the mains plug, it must be replaced with another 5 amp fuse. If you don't have one available, stop computing until you do. Fitting a 13 amp fuse, or none at all, risks serious damage and invalidates your guarantee.

 Don't use the wrong fuse.

Restarting your PC

Sooner or later you will want to restart your PC immediately after switching it off - perhaps you forgot to check some figures or print a letter...

Make sure that you follow the same start up procedure as usual. Hard disk users are advised to wait thirty seconds after switching off before switching on; you must be absolutely certain that your disk drive has stopped spinning completely before starting it up again. Ignoring this is one of the quickest ways to wreck a hard disk. In general, if you are at all likely to need your hard disk PC again later in the day, it will suffer less wear and tear if you leave it running.

 Never switch on your PC with a floppy disk in a disk drive

Don't use the mains switch on the wall socket instead of your PC on-off switch

Make sure a hard disk has stopped spinning completely before starting it up again

 Follow the correct startup procedure carefully every time

DISASTER CAUSE NUMBER 2 : Stopping

Just as road accidents often happen near the end of long journeys, PC users are also prone to mishaps, especially at the end of a long session: 'thank goodness that report/budget/forecast/chapter is finished - let's get out of here!'. There is a natural tendency, which must be resisted, just to switch off without more ado.

First of all, make sure that any data which you want to keep is saved on disk. Some programs, it is true, automatically save your files, while others at least remind you to do something - but some do not: you just have to remember.

 Always have at least one blank, formatted floppy disk available in case you miscalculate the space required for saving files

Your data might be in RAM (main memory); many spreadsheets, for example, keep data in RAM while you are manipulating it; they often do not remind you to save the sheet as a disk file. At other times, you might have vital data in a portion of RAM set aside as a RAM disk. In these cases, the data will behave just like a rapid-access disk file - until you switch off the PC, and realise that you have lost it all - RAM disk files disappear, like any other RAM data, when you take away the power. (The small area of 'non-volatile RAM' which is available to your Amstrad cannot be used for storing your data files.) We shall see later how to automate this saving process so that it becomes impossible to forget to do it.

Even if you have saved your data files onto disk several times during your computing session, which is highly advisable, you must still save them again when you want to finish, in order that you have the most up-to-date version stored on disk.

Your application program may give you an option to take an extra, backup copy of your files before you finally pack up. Use that option if available, to store backup copies on another disk; otherwise you can do it yourself by copying from GEM or DOS.

Never exit a program, or switch off your PC, without ensuring that your data is saved.

Secondly, you should always exit from the program in the correct manner. This may involve pressing 'Esc', 'F10' or some other key repeatedly, so as to go back through the menus which you have been using. Other programs may require you to type in 'Quit', 'End' or similar commands. There may even be some special end-of-day routines which must be carried out before leaving the program. Check the manual if you are unsure of the proper exit procedure.

The program may have to perform vital internal 'housekeeping' when you finish a session. It may be a matter of ensuring that files are properly closed. Sometimes there are control records or special counters (which you never actually see) to be updated. If this final tidying up is curtailed by some 'shortcut', the program may fail to work properly - or at all - the next time it is run.

Don't emulate 'expert' users who you may have seen switching off or resetting their machines, apparently in the middle of a program. They may sometimes get away with it; it is never worth the risk. I recommend that you exit all the way to the DOS prompt (A> or B> or C>) when you are finishing a computing session. If you are running a GEM-based application, then at least exit to the Desktop.

Thirdly, having ensured that any data you want to keep is saved on disk, and having exited the program in the correct way, ensure that any floppy disk is removed from the drive(s) and stored carefully before you finally switch off.

 Never shortcut the method of exiting from a program

Never switch off your PC with a floppy disk in a drive

Don't use the mains switch on the wall socket to switch off your PC

When you do finally want to end a computing session, switch off your PC and any peripherals, one at a time - pausing for a second or two between each - before switching off at the mains and *not* the other way round.

 Take your time when switching off

DISASTER CAUSE NUMBER 3 : Hardware Failure

Real hardware failures are most unusual; your Amstrad, like all well-designed PCs, is a remarkably reliable piece of equipment. Most apparent hardware failures are the result of failing to take simple preventative precautions. Occasionally, however, problems occur which are virtually impossible to prevent.

Disk problems

As with most systems, the moving parts are the least reliable: the most common physical problem is a disk drive fault. The read-write heads (the parts which 'fly' above and below the spinning disk surface to record or retrieve data) of a floppy disk drive periodically require cleaning. Your PC may warn you repeatedly that it cannot read or write to the drive in question. Otherwise, the symptoms could be several instances of corrupted data files giving you strange results. Typical warning messages which the system may display are listed in your Amstrad manual. Your dealer will recommend a cleaning method suitable for your machine.

If cleaning fails to remedy the problem, the heads may have become misaligned, or some other disk drive fault may have occurred. You can obtain (from most user groups or computer dealers) a disk containing programs to try to diagnose the problem. They are easy to run and can be informative. By all means find out what you can in this way, but do not assume that rectifying the fault will be as easy: leave such problems for your dealer to tackle.

Don't attempt to dismantle any part of your PC system, as this will invalidate your warranty.

Memory failure

When you switch on your PC, it goes through a number of checks, including a memory check. Very, very rarely it may fail this check, because one of its memory chips has failed. Equally unusual are cases where the PC appears to startup normally but actually has a memory fault.

This might show up as inconsistent behaviour, such as losing records, failing to find files which are apparently there, making inaccurate calculations, or program failures. Do not jump to the conclusion that you have a memory fault; it remains the least likely explanation. It is, I am afraid, much more probable that the record was deleted by mistake, the file had been corrupted, the input data was wrong or the program had a bug.

But how can you tell for sure? More technically-minded users can write a program to test their PC's RAM; other readers will be pleased to know that several such programs already exist. If your dealer cannot let you have a copy, you can obtain a suitable program from one of the PC user groups, for the cost of a disk plus a small handling charge. It will test every nook and cranny of your RAM in a couple of minutes, usually providing reassurance that all is well.

Other programs are available to check for all sorts of errors, for anyone with the time and the patience for them. Most readers are best advised to contact their dealers if they have real evidence of memory failure.

Burn-In

If you use your PC to run the *same* program for several hours each day, the continued display of one specific screen layout (menus, commands, ruler lines etc.) can cause burn-in, physically etching the letters or symbols into the screen.

This danger is minimised by keeping the screen intensity reasonably low - and virtually eliminated by running a special utility program in conjunction with your usual application. This will blank out the screen if no keys are pressed for a certain period of time. Pressing any key (the Shift key is best as it will not enter anything into the PC) will 'wake up' the display.

Processor Failure

I have never come across a case of failure of the central processor of a microcomputer. Still, I suppose there's a first time for everything... Generally speaking, your hardware, properly treated, is most unlikely to let you down.

DISASTER CAUSE NUMBER 4 : Other Hardware Problems

Loose connections

The most common cause of apparent hardware failure is a simple loose connection. When you set up the most basic PC 1512 or 1640 system, you have a minimum of five plugs to insert. Most users will install a printer, adding at least three more plugs to their collection. Each one must be gently but firmly pushed home. The power plug itself must be properly wired and be fitted with a 5 amp fuse.

Give some thought to the location of your PC, making sure that nobody can trip over any of the cables. This precaution will protect your PC, passers-by and you! If such an accident does occur, it can also cause serious problems with insurance policies. If you are supervising an employee who trips up, you can be charged (not your boss, you!) under the Health and Safety at Work Act.

 Don't let your cables get intertwined: interference can pass between them, especially if they are not well shielded

It is worth quickly checking all the plugs and connections each day before starting up your system. Bear in mind that vibration, such as that from an impact printer, can actually shake a plug (or even a chip) loose over time; therefore the clips or screws built into some plugs should be carefully tightened (but not too far). Impact printers should not share a desk with your PC if you can avoid it.

Do read the manual of any printer or other peripheral device carefully; there may be several cables to connect: power, data, even an earth lead sometimes. I still remember with some embarrassment an occasion several years ago, when I spent half an hour struggling to make a sheet feeder work properly with a daisywheel printer, in order to print a large batch of letters. It had worked perfectly the previous day, but now the paper kept feeding to different heights: Dear Mr Bloggs was halfway down the page, while Dear Miss Smith was lost in the letterheading. Power was obviously reaching both devices, so no problem with the plugs - obviously. I tried every combination of settings, altered the paper lengths, issued esoteric command sequences, to no avail. Then, at last, I checked: someone had pulled out the plug between the feeder and the printer!

PHYSICAL FITNESS FOR YOUR PC

There are a number of precautions which can be taken to keep your PC system in first class physical condition, despite the hazards of the typical office or home environment.

Heat and Damp

High temperatures and high humidity are not normally among the problems faced by UK users. But some people work in artificially over-heated or (rarely) steamy offices; their PCs are likely to suffer. Locate your PC sensibly, in a reasonably cool and completely dry spot - and, on the rare occasions when we do get a real heatwave in the UK, keep your computer cool. If that is impossible, just don't use it: a burnt-out chip could be expensive to identify and replace. Extremes of temperature, like vibration, can actually loosen chips in their sockets. Don't let your PC get too cold, either.

Dust and Dirt

Obviously your PC will play up if you supply a dusty, dirty environment. Avoid fluffy carpets if at all possible, dust and vacuum clean regularly. It is far better to remove dust with a damp cloth than to redistribute it with the traditional feather duster, which is sure to send the dust homing in unerringly on your PC! The PC itself, particularly the screen and keyboard, will attract plenty of dust anyway; a dustcover designed to fit is inexpensive and strongly recommended. The dustcover itself should be wiped occasionally, otherwise it could do more harm than good.

If you fear that dust may have entered your PC casing, you can clean inside with a special compressed air can, gently wiping the components with a sable brush. Switch off the power and unplug the PC before removing the cover.

 Don't let your PC get too hot, too cold, damp, dusty or dirty.

Static Electricity

Static is a key reason for dust problems and is itself a major hazard. It can corrupt disks, disrupt memory contents and even damage chips. With synthetic clothing and, especially, carpets you are likely to build up a high 'personal' charge, the release of which can cause havoc. If you are furnishing an office from scratch, consider using special carpet designed to minimise static charge. Screens and keyboards are also prone to static buildup - and the shrink-wrapping around some software packages on the market is not exactly helpful.

Wiping the system with a very slightly damp cloth will help; special anti-static spray and/or 'wipes' are better. Users themselves should be earthed: just touching a radiator may help to dissipate any charge. The best solution is to invest in an anti-static mat, permanently wired to earth; this sits under the PC, or (the larger type) on the floor beneath the user. Most dealers and suppliers of 'consumables' (paper, ribbons, disks, etc.) will be able to sell you such a mat.

If you own a PC 1512 and have decided to increase your RAM to 640K, and are planning to insert the extra memory chips yourself (see the Appendix for sources) - two warnings:

Never handle a chip without carefully earthing yourself

Don't forget that you may violate your warranty by making any hardware modification

Power Problems

A normal 240 volt AC supply fluctuates quite a bit; occasionally a power 'surge' or 'spike' occurs which could seriously trouble your PC and, in the worst case, permanently damage it. Any power-hungry equipment being switched on or off on the same ring main can cause similar problems. The manager of one small company could never fathom out why their PC screen blanked out every Thursday morning; it didn't take too long to discover that their cleaning-lady came round on Thursdays, switching her vacuum cleaner on in the next-door office! Even switching a printer on can sometimes cause quite a jolt in the ring mains.

'Surge protectors' can be obtained to guard against these mishaps. You can obtain quite a sophisticated box of electronics, with battery backup to guarantee continuous, smooth power - even for an hour or two after a power cut. At the other end of the scale an inexpensive modified plug is available; this will reduce electrical 'noise', protect against spikes and surges - but obviously not against power cuts. These latter devices give reasonable protection for most PC applications.

When buying a surge protector, check its specification. It should be able to absorb 5000 volts or more and should have a response time of no more than 10 nanoseconds (10 millionths of a second).

Save your data files regularly, during as well as at the end of a computing session

A different type of power problem can arise if you overload your PC with add-on hardware; all the power for an Amstrad PC is drawn from the transformer in the monitor unit. The type of hard disk which is actually on an expansion card can be fitted to your PC, but is quite thirsty for power, especially if it is competing for its supply with other add-on cards in adjacent expansion slots. Check with your dealer before installing these devices.

Spillages

In an ideal world you would never have a drink or other liquid anywhere near your PC. If you cannot leave your PC to take a coffee break then at least ensure that you have enough desk space to reduce the risk, and do keep drinks well away from disk drives. Remember that your Amstrad power cable does not have a separate earth lead; although the output voltage is low, there is still a hazard. If you do spill anything, the chances are that it will be over the keyboard. This should not be disastrous: unplug it, sponge it carefully and leave it to dry naturally; it will probably be as good as new.

Take precautions against static electricity, power problems and liquid spillage

Check your batteries occasionally; if they show the slightest signs of leakage, replace them immediately

DISASTER CAUSE NUMBER 5 : Disk Failure

Hardware, of course, includes disks - but disk problems are so common that they deserve a section of their very own. There are many potential hazards to floppy disks:

Don't let disks get dusty, too hot (radiators, sunshine) or too cold.

Don't touch the exposed surfaces or allow them to rest on anything; the only thing they should contact is their paper envelopes or the disk drive itself.

Don't expose disks to liquids or magnetic fields (don't put them close to your monitor, TV, telephone, etc.).

Magnetic 'executive toys' with paperclips, ball bearings etc. have quite a powerful enough field to wreck a floppy disk. If you have to travel by air with floppy disks, don't let them get within several feet of either the X-ray machines or the metal detector gates. Don't accept official blandishments that these devices are not harmful.

 Don't apply any pressure to disks: don't put anything on top of them, don't write on the label once it is stuck on (except, if necessary, very gently with a soft fibre-tipped pen), don't bend them, don't cram them into a storage box (buy another one).

Don't insert or remove a disk from a drive until the green light is out (if you really cannot wait those few seconds you can even buy a program to reduce the delay before the light goes out!).

Don't (as we've said before) switch your PC on or off with any floppy disks in the drive(s).

One final hazard is smoke. Again, you will hear tales of chain-smoking PC users who have never had a disk problem since 1926 - but smoke particles, though not always quite as big as dust particles, are of significant size compared to the tracks on a disk. The cunning little things can even penetrate the supposedly hermetical sealing of a hard disk drive, and cause trouble within. We have already discussed the problem of dirty read-write heads on the drive itself, which can physically score the disk surface.

 Don't use anything other than a recommended cleaning kit for your floppy disk drives.

If damage has occurred to a floppy disk, it really isn't worth trying to salvage it or use the undamaged area: retrieve and copy what you can, then throw it away. More about salvage in the next chapter.

Disk discipline

Try to get into the habit of always putting the disk straight back into its envelope, and its storage box, when you have finished with it. You may already have discovered my Law of Floppy Disk Envelopes, which states that:

When n floppy disks are in use, the number of floppy disk envelopes available is always less than or equal to (n-1).

 Keep the envelopes themselves in the appropriate disk box, at the front; this not only stops them from sneaking under your keyboard, inside your manuals, etc., but also keeps the envelopes themselves dust-free.

 When you start using a new program, never be tempted to start using the master disk ("I'll take a backup later, when I've got the hang of it..."). Always take a backup straight away, and store the master(s) safely elsewhere.

Disk reliability

Having advised all this caution, perhaps some reassurance is called for: floppy disks really are very reliable these days. Two more suggestions to increase your safety margin:

 Buy top-quality, double-sided, double density floppy disks (you can get them at a fair price from PC user groups, etc.). The extra couple of pounds per box is well worth it: they are better made, more thoroughly tested, have reinforced centre holes and tougher envelopes.

When you use disks regularly, day after day, e.g. your startup disks, or your word processing program disk, the wear and tear must ultimately tell. Pension them off after say, two or three years; copy them and use the fresh copy before trouble occurs.

You should always write the date on the disk label when you first use the disk. To be doubly sure you can also store a magnetic label (up to 20 characters) on a floppy disk when you format it by using the /V switch, keying in, say, FORMAT B: /V ENTER. The system will then ask you to type in your label; thereafter the label will be displayed on screen whenever you look at the disk directory.

Hard disks

Hard disks are even safer than floppies. When originally formatted, it is quite normal to find a number of unusable sectors. This is not a cause for concern, as the operating system avoids trying to write to or read from these areas, and the disk is built with extra space to allow for these slight imperfections.

If you haven't already done so, it is worth taking a few minutes to update your main User Instructions Manual according to the amendments in Appendix HD1 of the Hard Disk Installation Instructions. (1640 owners already have one combined manual).

There has been some debate as to whether HD machines suffer from overheating, especially with extra cards (e.g. for networking) installed in expansion slots. The publicity generated was enough to persuade Amstrad to fit a fan in later hard disk versions. The results of the (independent) tests which I have seen suggested that the temperatures inside the casing remained well within acceptable tolerances. So there is no cause for alarm if you have an earlier HD computer. All the same, there is no need to locate your PC on top of a radiator; it will be happiest well away from any heat source - including direct sunlight.

Moving your PC

Hard disks in particular do not like unnecessary travel. Keep the original packing, and move any PC (especially HD models) with care. This applies even for moving a machine within your office. You may also be able to get hold of a utility program to 'park' the read/write heads before transit.

DISASTER CAUSE NUMBER 6 : Formatting

Remember that formatting deletes any files on the disk. Check carefully that you have specified the correct disk. Fortunately, formatting disasters are less common than they used to be, as MS-DOS now insists that you say which drive you want formatted. If you have specified your hard disk, you will get a stern warning and a chance to abort the procedure before it is too late.

GEM also requires you to choose which disk to format, by clicking on that disk's icon, before pulling down the File menu and selecting format. GEM then shows a Dialog box to give you a last chance to change your mind.

Used with care, the formatting procedure should not cause trouble. If you want to protect yourself or colleagues (perhaps your secretary - or your boss) from the risk of formatting the wrong disk, there are several possible approaches:

1) Tell people not to do it. This will fail: people are always curious, and often careless, especially when under pressure.
2) You can create 'command files' to force FORMAT commands to work only on the disk drive(s) of your choice. This is rather fiddly, though, and not foolproof. We will see later (chapter 8) how to set up command files for various purposes.
3) It is simpler just to rename the FORMAT command files (note that two are supplied with your system: FORMAT.COM and FORMAT.EXE). We saw how to rename files in the last chapter. Calling them something completely obscure like QX54GBE5.COM may help but somebody might still get curious - "funny looking command - wonder what it does?...". Better to drop the filetypes .COM or .EXE; then the command cannot be directly executed.
4) Simplest and perhaps even better is removal of the risky commands. Having copied them onto a floppy disk which is kept well away from the PC (in a safe if available), simply delete the FORMAT commands.

 To eliminate the risk of formatting the wrong disk, remove all FORMAT commands from your working disks. Hard disk users should never leave the HDFORMAT program sitting on their PCs.

DISASTER CAUSE NUMBER 7 : Copying Files

Copying files can cause minor problems; for example, if the target disk is too full (see disaster cause number 9 below) the copy will fail. However, the system will warn you of the difficulty, it will not usually leave fragments of files on your disks, and the problem is usually remedied by clearing some space, or selecting another disk, and trying the copy again.

Real trouble can arise from inadvertently copying in the wrong direction. Suppose you wanted to take a backup copy of your accounts master file ACCTMAST, which is on the drive you normally use - let's say C. You want the copy on a backup floppy disk which you have placed in drive A. Now, what happens if you type in: COPY A:ACCTMAST ENTER ? If you're lucky, nothing. However, if you had a previous copy of ACCTMAST on the floppy disk, that file will be copied from drive A onto drive C (assuming that is the default drive), obliterating the up-to-date version of ACCT-MAST!

Remember that the first filename you give in the COPY command is taken to be the source file i.e. the file you are copying FROM. The second name is the destination file i.e. the file you are copying TO. If you omit this second name, the system assumes you want to keep the name the same, and tries to copy the file onto the current default drive.

One way of completing the above copying operation without mishap is to key in: COPY C:ACCTMAST A:ACCTMAST (no harm in spelling out the name twice), which will copy the up-to-date ACCTMAST file from drive C to drive A.

Better still, give the backup copy a better name. Why not say something like: COPY C:ACCTMAST A:ACCMAS01.88. By using a unique and meaningful name for the copied file in this way, your copying operation is safeguarded and you have a better chance of knowing which backup file to use when, should the need arise.

 Take care to specify both disk drives and both filenames when copying. Use meaningful names for files to avoid confusion

If you are running GEM-based applications, and therefore copy files from the GEM Desktop, these risks are reduced, as GEM will advise you of any name conflict during copying.

Any readers used to CP/M may have used PIP (which is a DOS - Plus command available to 1512 users) to copy files in the past. You may recall, and should beware that PIP, unlike COPY, expects the DESTINATION file FIRST. I suggest that you leave this rather 'user-hostile' command in the past where it belongs.

 Don't copy files in the wrong direction

DISASTER CAUSE NUMBER 8 : Overwriting Files

Careless COPYing is not the only way in which vital files can be overwritten. Most applications programs offer you the option of saving your data to a disk file; it is, of course, advisable to exercise this option at regular intervals during, as well as at the end of, a computing session.

Imagine we are watching a Hardworking, but Disaster-Prone, PC user finish work for the day. He remembers that he must save his data, so he selects Save, and the program replies with something like:

Save as ...? Please Enter Filename or press ENTER for directory

He cannot be bothered to check the directory, and it is late. He has just created a small table of figures, so he keys in the obvious filename: FIGURES and hits ENTER a couple of times. (You may have noticed that you can sometimes get an unintentional double-strike of a key on the Amstrad keyboard.)

Our hapless user has just destroyed his company's entire budget for next year.... A minute later, he remembers: it took him days of toil to finalise and he saved it as.... you guessed it: FIGURES! The second press of the ENTER key told the program to overwrite the existing FIGURES file; this program did at least warn him that a file of that name was already on the default disk. Some programs do not even warn you: they will just overwrite any existing file. You do not have to be utterly careless to overwrite a file by mistake; it is a relatively easy error to make.

 Whenever you create or save a file, check whether the file already exists. If so, satisfy yourself that you are happy to dispense with its contents before you overwrite it.

Keeping track of files

If you always know the name, location and contents of each file, you are far less likely to overwrite a file by mistake. But nobody can be expected to remember all that information - so don't try. You should keep a log of what is stored where.

The more meaningful your filenames are, the more 'self-document-ing' they become, but directories alone are not enough, because they do not tell you any detail about the file contents. Use a system that you are comfortable with; here are some options.

1) Keep a log book, perhaps with a page for each disk. Columns should include filename, time and date created, who created it (if there is more than one user of the PC), and description of contents. For instance:

DISK NO: PAY004

Date	Time	User	Filename(s)	Created	Updated	Deleted	Contents/Notes
20/1/88	1730	JKA	88MSUM.RPT	✓			YEAR END SUMMARY PAYROLL REPORT
1/2/88	1000	JKA	CT8801.TRN	✓			JANUARY SUBCONTR. TIMESHEETS
5/2/88	1905	TM	YR87.MF	(BACKUP ON BK007)		✓	1987 PAYROLL MASTER DELETED AFTER AUDIT

Possible layout for a PC file log book

If a new file is created, a new line is written on the log. If it overwrites/replaces a previous version, the line describing the original file can simply be crossed out. You could add columns for further details for deletions, renaming, backups, etc. but it is better to keep the log simple and quick to use. A separate log for backups is recommended (see disaster cause no. 18 below). If this seems like hard work, we'll look at ways of automating such logs in chapter 8.

2) Alternatively, keep an annotated directory listing for each floppy disk. You can print such a list quite easily (see Chapter 7) or use an inexpensive program written especially for the job, which will print a neat disk-sized directory which can be slipped into the protective envelope. Obviously, hard disk users will need a ring binder or a box file to keep such records, perhaps with a section for each folder or directory on the disk.

The programs mentioned above will also print neat disk labels with directory details. The problems with these are (a) even though they use condensed print (which may limit the printers you can use) they get rather cluttered and you cannot add any comment about file contents, and (b) if your files change fairly regularly, you will keep on having to replace the labels, which is dangerous for your disks.

Clearly, no system will be of any use in keeping track of your data unless you keep it up to date.

 Keep a separate, up-to-date, written, log of your data files

Write protection of files

You can prevent any file from being overwritten by write protecting them. If using GEM, click on the icon of the file you want to protect, pull down the File menu and select Information/Rename. In the Dialog box which appears (see the screen display on page 40) change the Attributes to Read-Only (by pointing and clicking). Click on OK, and the file is now protected from being overwritten, changed or deleted by mistake. Any attempt to delete a Read-Only file will fail.

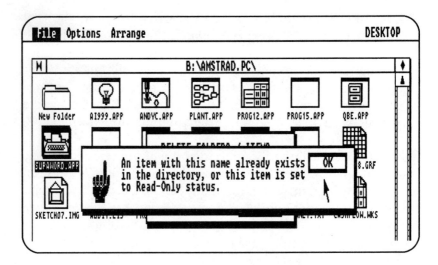

GEM refusing to delete a Read-Only program file

To remove the protection, repeat the process, clicking on Read/ Write instead. As usual, you can do the same job of protecting or unprotecting files directly from MS-DOS if this is more convenient. To prevent a file from being written to, use the MS-DOS command ATTRIB. For example:

ATTRIB + R VITAL.DAT will make the VITAL.DAT file read-only, so that it can be examined and used but not edited, modified, overwritten or deleted. To reverse the process:

ATTRIB -R VITAL.DAT will allow VITAL.DAT to be read or written to - or overwritten or deleted!

Write protection of floppy disks

A whole floppy disk can be protected by covering the write-protect notch (the quarter-inch notch in the top-righthand edge) with a small sticky label. With the notch covered, nothing can be written to the disk (this is also useful for making certain that you never copy in the wrong direction). It is unwise to leave these labels on for long, though; after a few months they tend to come unstuck, get caught when you are inserting or removing the disk, and worst of all, can fall off inside the disk drive. If you want to ensure that several files cannot be written over, use the ATTRIB command instead. Hard disk users have no choice.

Change a file's attributes (using GEM or the MS-DOS ATTRIB command) to Read-Only to protect any vital data from being overwritten

Don't leave write-protect tabs on floppy disks for too long

DISASTER CAUSE NUMBER 9 : Deleting Files

Much of the above applies equally to accidental deletion of the wrong file. Careful naming of files, keeping a record of what data is stored where and when, write protection where appropriate - all these techniques will reduce the risk.

Remember that the files shown by the DIR command, or the icons displayed in a GEM window, are those on the default drive/directory only. If there is more than one directory on a disk, the missing file might be in a different directory. This could have arisen, for example, by running a program which was not in the default directory at the time. The program may appear to run normally, but may still write files to the default directory, rather than its own.

Therefore, do not jump to the conclusion that a file has been deleted without carefully checking:

Have you got the name absolutely correct?
Including the filetype, if any, after a full stop?
Are you looking on the right disk and/or disk drive?
The right directory/folder?
Has the file been copied? Renamed?
Is there a backup copy?

Wildcards, remember, as well as being useful for copying and looking at directories, are terribly efficient for deleting files. If you key in DEL *.* ENTER, the system will ask you if you are sure (from which disk will that command delete everything? That's right, whichever is the default drive at the moment). However DEL *.DOC ENTER will delete every file of filetype DOC *without* asking you if you are sure.

Don't use wildcards to delete files unless you are certain

Unauthorised Users

If you are working with several other people, you might want to take precautions to prevent their deleting your files, whether by design or accident. You might consider locking up your PC and/or important data, password controls for access to some or all of your systems. Space does not permit a thorough discussion of security issues in this book, but bear in mind that:

 Unauthorised users may inadvertently or deliberately delete your files

DISASTER CAUSE NUMBER 10 : Full Disks and Directories

Unless you keep an eye on how full your disks are getting, the first warning you get may be the sight of your program crashing, which is usually too late.

Some programs nowadays do check disk space for you, and warn you that there is not enough room to store the file you wish to keep. Even this safeguard is useless unless the program also allows you to copy and/or delete some files to clear some space without leaving the program. You will of course lose any un-saved files if you have to leave the program. I know it sounds unlikely, but it happens to somebody every day.

When is a Disk full?

We have already seen how to find out the size of a file, and the space left on a disk, with GEM or DOS. The better-designed applications programs have the ability to show you how much space is on a disk while you are working, without having to exit to GEM or DOS. One way or another, you must always have an idea of how much room is left.

Don't start running a program which may create or add to disk files without checking on disk space first

Let us observe another working session with our Disaster-Prone User. He has decided to make some additions to a report which he has been compiling, so he is just about to start his word processing program running when he remembers: "I must check my disk space...".

The check reveals that there are 16,384 bytes (i.e. characters) available on disk, so there is no problem, he says to himself, as he is going to add no more than a page or two, say 5,000 bytes at most to the report.

He takes several hours polishing his prose and is pretty well pleased at the results. Now, just save it, print a couple of copies and call it a day. Select Save, and.....

ERROR: diskette is full

The user sits blinking at the screen; it blinks back:

A>

having 'bombed' out of the word processing program. All is not quite lost; the original version of the report is probably still there - but four hours' editing is lost.

Editing Space

Why was his calculation so wrong? In order for a word processor (or any other editing program) to enable you to make changes to a document, it must have not only a copy of the original document (usually on disk) but *also* enough free space to create an entire new version of the document, *not* just room for the additions.

In our poor user's case, the original report was some 40,000 bytes in size, so there should have been at least 50,000 bytes free to stand any chance of a successful edit.

Once again, some programs will not allow you to start editing a file unless there is ample space for the original and edited versions on disk (plus, sometimes, extra work space!) - but they are by no means the rule. So, be extremely generous with spare disk space, perhaps especially so with floppy disks. A floppy on your Amstrad PC (at the time of writing) holds a maximum of 360,000 bytes. As a general rule:

 Never let the free space for data files on a floppy disk get below 50,000 bytes

Even that is too little if you make a habit of storing giant files. It really is a terrible false economy to try to jam pack your disks. You may have noticed that some of your systems or program disks cut it a bit fine; that's OK, because in normal circumstances you should never be trying to store any more files on them.

If you find your hard disk getting below 1,000,000 characters of free space, it is time to suspend normal operations and carry out a careful, but nonetheless ruthless, spring cleaning operation.

 Never let the free space on a hard disk get below 1,000,000 (yes, one million!) bytes

 Always leave ample room for editing files, plus a generous safety zone, on your disks

Full Directories

Another ominous message which may be encountered, even though you have made sure that there is loads of space on your disk, is:

Warning - directory full

If you have stored a large number of small files on a disk there may not be room for any more files in the directory itself (although most users will run out of disk space before they run out of directory entries). The number of possible directory/folder entries depends on the disk; for double-sided floppies the limit is normally 112 entries. If you run up against this limit in the middle of processing, you could be in trouble - unless you can copy/delete files without exiting. To avoid this problem, simply set up subdirectories (new folders) within the main (root) directory. If you really need to, you can set up subdirectories within subdirectories, allowing you a huge number of directory entries.

Don't keep on adding files to your disks without checking on the total number of files in the directory

Before nearing the limit on directory entries, reorganise your disk and/or set up a new subdirectory

DISASTER CAUSE NUMBER 11 : Printing

Printing tends to produce many niggly problems; Chapter 7 is devoted to the subject. But when do printing problems cause 'disasters', as we have defined the term? There are two main types of printing disaster, both really due to poor software design; both can be guarded against.

Printing without a printer

This process, as you might guess, is difficult. What happens is that the user asks the system (intentionally or accidentally) to start printing something - but there is no printer available. The user may think there is a printer available, but perhaps it is not switched on, not plugged in properly, not 'on-line' (i.e. ready to receive and print data from the computer), out of paper, and so on. As far as the PC is concerned, the printer does not exist.

The result depends on the program you are using. If the program actually checks the printer status, it may be able to warn the user with a message like "Please check printer". Otherwise, the program may just 'hang', with the screen frozen. Occasionally, correcting the printer problem will free the system without damage; more often, though, it is too late. Yet again, any file in use at the time is likely to be lost. Many popular data base, word processing and accounting programs fail to protect you from this mishap.

The precautions are obvious. If there is the remotest chance that you might want to print something at any stage in your computing session, ensure that your printer is properly connected, switched on, on-line and ready to print. Furthermore, and I shall keep on nagging about this, save your information on disk at regular intervals.

 Don't start a computing session without checking the state of your printer

While we are on the subject, a warning for anyone programming in BASIC-2 who may be more used to other versions of the language. Bear in mind that the LIST command does not list your program on the screen (in the EDIT window), but prints it on the printer. With no printer attached, BASIC-2 freezes.

Printing mishaps

Similar problems can occur when something goes wrong in the middle of printing e.g. the paper snarls up, someone accidentally pulls the plug on the printer. Often you can just abandon printing, set the printer up properly and start again. However, the worst-behaved programs can crash in these circumstances with possible data loss.

There are even packages which will not let you repeat a printout, even though the report you obtained first time is useless! I tested, quite recently, an accounting package which allowed one shot only at the month end reports. If you forgot to replace that printer ribbon - jolly bad luck - wait until next month! The company assured me that their imminent new release would correct the problem. Don't believe such promises until you see them fulfilled. Printing problems are covered more fully in Chapter 7.

DISASTER CAUSE NUMBER 12 : 'Warmstarts'

Occasionally your PC will 'hang' for no apparent reason; it will not respond to any normal key depression. The only answer is to 'warmstart' it, i.e. to reset the machine by holding down the Ctrl and Alt keys while pressing the Del key at the bottom righthand corner of your keyboard. Any data in memory, including any files on RAM Disk, or files being edited, will be lost.

The cause (if not disconnected printer as above) is usually a program bug; all programs, except the most trivial, contain bugs. They may be 'known' bugs for which the software developer may have found a solution (probably not much help now) or unknown ones which can simply lurk in the program, sometimes for years, waiting to afflict the unsuspecting user.

If your program does 'hang' for no obvious reason, write down straight away exactly what you were doing, the files you were using and the last few commands which you had typed in. The more detail you can record at the time, the more likely it is that your program manual, your dealer or the software company will be able to help. With luck, you may find that you have made a simple error, and the manual will help you out of trouble. If you are very lucky indeed, (a) you will manage to get through to a 'hotline' support number, and (b) they will tell you exactly how to 'unfreeze' your PC. But don't count on it.

Accidentally pressing the wrong keys can sometimes lock up your system in this way; the software should of course protect you from such accidents, but all too often it will not. A common example (which is really another printing problem) is the PrtSc key (Shift and *) which will lock your system unless your printer is attached and ready.

 In case your system 'freezes' and you have to restart it, save your data files to disk at regular intervals

DISASTER CAUSE NUMBER 13 : Program Crashes

A similar, but sometimes more dramatic, event is a program actually 'crashing'; this can sometimes dump you right out to DOS. The result as before is loss of any data or files you were in the middle of using, often including any files on RAM Disk.

Programs crashing or hanging may give rise to further problems: there may be temporary files used by the program, which are normally merged with others and/or deleted at the end. Other files may not be closed properly; special control records may not be updated, and so on. In other words, this is similar to disaster cause number 2, exiting the program in the wrong way. But a program crash, of course, is impossible to control or correct.

Some programs are so delicate that they will crash if you, say, enter an 'O' when you meant to enter a '0'. These elementary failings are now rare but many programs can still be crashed by invalid data, or sometimes by data which is of the wrong order of magnitude.

 Check that data is reasonable and valid before keying it in

Other common causes of crashes:

Bad hardware connections (e.g. mouse, keyboard, printer): make sure plugs are firmly in their sockets before starting

Missing files: check which files your program needs; ensure they are available

Wrong path/directory specified: if applicable, check that the system knows where to look for files, or where to put them

Wrong version of operating system: if a program has been set up to run under MS-DOS version 3.2, running it under a different version or under DOS-Plus will probably annoy it.

Trying to write to or replace a read-only disk or file: if in doubt, check the data disk and/or the attributes of the file(s) concerned.

DISASTER CAUSE NUMBER 14 : Incorrect Commands

Although incorrect commands are usually inconvenient rather than disastrous, we have seen some examples of more serious cases: formatting the wrong disk, deleting too many files, copying in the wrong direction, etc. These tend to be mistakes made in using the more powerful DOS commands, but grave errors can also be made by entering the wrong commands within an applications program.

One day our Disaster-Prone User is beavering away, reconstructing the spreadsheet data he accidentally obliterated (see Disaster Cause No. 8 above). He makes a small slip, entering a figure into the wrong 'cell'.
"No problem", he thinks, "I can easily blank that entry out.... Now, what was the command? Oh, yes, I just say Zap, and hit ENTER, and ..."
He has destroyed his entire spreadsheet again!

A few weeks later, having finally triumphed over his budgets (they used to be so much quicker by hand...), he has turned his attention to word processing again. He has spent much of the day editing a lengthy report. Having been too engrossed to save any of the changes he has made to the document during the day, he remembers that he must quickly save it now before packing up and going home.
"Let me see, now... get out of editing, and save the file... I'll print it in the morning..." So he keys Q to quit edit, and the computer replies:
"Abandon edited version of C:REPORT66 (Y/N) ?"
"Yes, yes, I told you, I want to abandon editing and then save the document..." he mutters to the computer, and keys in Y for yes.
"Hurry up, or I'll miss the 5.57..." he adds.
"Abandoning edited version of C:REPORT66"
replies the computer. One whole day's work down the tubes again!

In the first case, of course, he shouldn't have used the Zap command on his spreadsheet (the command he wanted was Blank), while in the second example he wanted to abandon edit*ing*, but in his haste he told the PC to chuck away the edit*ed* version of his document i.e. all the additions and changes that he had made during the day.

Ridiculous mistakes you'd never make? I very much hope you are right, but the lessons are clear. Never guess what to key in. Take your time, check that you are using the right commands and check that you are using them correctly. Punctuation and spelling mistakes, which you might get away with in normal circumstances, can wreak havoc on your PC data.

 Don't try to guess how to key in commands; get them right. Use help from the screen, the manual, fellow users, dealers - anywhere

The information should be immediately available. Most programs now have extensive help screens which you can display even when you are right in the middle of keying in a command. (They are usually brought on to the screen by pressing the F1 key.) If the help screens are inadequate, go back to the manual (which you studied anyway before you started using the package) and make sure you know what you are doing.

If you are still in the dark, get hold of a friend, colleague, dealer, consultant, software vendor - anybody who can help to explain what to do next. Don't be embarrassed to ask about what may be a simple point; in any case, a slight embarrassment is preferable to the disaster you may cause if you just guess.

Many PC users find it helpful to keep their own 'personal' manual for all the programs/systems they use. This explains in their own words the sequence of commands to use in given circumstances and the reasons why. You may prefer to write notes on the printed manual to clarify matters; after all, you've paid for it, it's not sacrosanct, just another tool for you to use.

 Compile your own 'user manual' or similar aide-memoire explaining commands and useful operations in your own words. Otherwise, annotate the official user manual for your program to clarify it where necessary.

DISASTER CAUSE NUMBER 15 : Memory Full

It is strange to recall now that the first home microcomputers were equipped with 1 (one) K of memory; the variety and ingenuity of programs which could be crammed into those machines was almost unbelievable. In the commercial world, machines with a giant 64K of memory (not all usable) soon became the norm: a standard reinforced by the advent of the IBM PC.

In five years, the typical PC's memory has multiplied tenfold, yet the exponential growth in PC software available has made it even easier to fill up the space. For the Amstrad user with an unexpanded 512K machine, the two main culprits are GEM, and the RAM Disk (for users with only floppy disks).

If you are running GEM with all the Desktop accessories available as well as using a RAM disk, it is quite easy to run out of memory. In fact you cannot have a RAM disk larger than 34K if you want it to coexist with your Desktop and an applications program.

Many best-selling programs in fact require more RAM than GEM normally likes to spare (you can specify this when configuring an application) while others recommend a larger RAM disk in order to improve performance. You may wish to use other programs which sit in RAM ready for instant action e.g. a diary manager, keyboard enhancer programs, 'on-line' spelling checker or Thesaurus. Such programs can be called up from within another program at the touch of a key, and after use will return you to exactly where you left off. Whether you are using these or other RAM-hungry programs, sooner or later you will run out of memory.

Only rarely will this signify disaster. It may mean you have to change the size of, or do without a RAM disk (see Chapter 8). It may mean that you cannot run under GEM, but must set up a special disk to load and run this particular program. It may force you to limit the size of certain files: many spreadsheets, graphics programs and some word processors (e.g. GEM Write) keep the current file entirely in RAM until you decide to save it.

All these can be tolerated, and even if you run out of memory while using a program, you will normally be warned, and have a chance to rectify matters (by reducing your data). But you may still encounter the badly-behaved package. Some programs will fail without warning if the user inadvertently fills all the available (RAM) memory.

You may not discover that your program has such bad manners until it is too late, but most RAM-dependent programs will tell you how much memory is left available for your data. If yours doesn't, you can try to test the limits with a jumbo file of nonsense which you don't mind losing.

Most users will have little difficulty in staying well under the limit for data in RAM for any given application. Always leave as large a margin as you can.

 Take care not to fill up all available RAM during processing

DISASTER CAUSE NUMBER 16 : Oversized Files

A large number of application programs operate in a way which does not require you to keep all your current data in RAM; they will read a manageable chunk from disk into RAM, allow you to process or manipulate it - and then write the changed data back to disk, before reading in another chunk. This enables some programs to handle extremely large files.

However, oversized files can still cause trouble, even if your program appears able to cope with them. Once again, a surprising number of programs begin to creak under the strain of all that data! In the worst cases, they may pack up, with the loss of the entire file.

The drawbacks of giant files are:

1. Occasional program failure without warning.

2. It is much easier to run out of disk space when editing and/or adding data to big files.

3. Editing and saving the file take significantly longer; if you are impatient you might exit from the program or switch off too quickly.

4. If disaster does strike, the size of the problem is proportional to the size of the file.

Take two common examples, word processing and accounting. If you let a word processed document on floppy disk get bigger than, say, 30 pages, the system can take more than a minute just to read through from top to bottom. This can be frustrating (time really drags when you are watching an operation like this on screen) and can in turn lead to careless mistakes. Some users understandably feel that they are losing one of the major advantages of word processing, simple and speedy editing. Hard disk users are unlikely to face this speed problem, but are equally vulnerable to loss of data if tempted to use very large files (drawback 4 above).

 Don't word process files much bigger than, say, 30 pages. Split larger documents into two or more files with different names

Accounts packages often keep one file containing all the transactions for the current period. In most cases, this file should be 'purged' at intervals - usually monthly. You can, however, sometimes get away with missing out this procedure, simply building up a giant transactions file for the whole year. The result is likely to be noticeably slower operation, as well as higher risk. If the file is corrupted for any reason, you could end up having to key in a whole year's data, instead of just a few weeks' worth.

There are of course some applications for which there is no alternative to using large files - but they are few and far between. As a general rule:

 Keep your data files as compact as you reasonably can. Carry out period end procedures, file purges etc. promptly so as to reduce data volumes

DISASTER CAUSE NUMBER 17 : Using the Wrong File(s)

It may be obvious when the wrong file has been selected for use: the figures are clearly incorrect, the letter or report is not what you wanted to edit, and so on. Trouble arises when you think you have the right file, because at first glance it seems to contain what you expected.

Word processed documents

The Disaster-Prone User, you will remember, is not always too fussy about his filenames. A week ago he spent several hours repeating the corrections and improvements to his report, which he had called REPORT66. As he had previously lost all his changes by a careless slip, he decided to save the edited version as REPORT66.NEW, before printing a draft copy for his boss to review. Today he has just received a lengthy memo with suggested changes from his boss. Better get them done PDQ - the final report must be at head office by Monday...

So he loads up REPORT66 and edits away for an hour or so. He is starting to accept, grudgingly, that some of these ideas do in fact improve the entire case, when he sees a clumsily phrased passage... "Surely I've already changed that?"
Indeed he has, and in the same moment he remembers that all his own changes were saved in REPORT66.NEW, not REPORT66. He may be able to salvage something by 'cutting and pasting' between the two files, but a lot of time has been wasted.

 Take care over your filenames. Always check that you are editing the correct file

Accounts files and spreadsheets

Here the plot thickens. Some accounts packages collect transactions together into batches, and require you periodically to update the master file(s) by submitting a whole batch of transactions in one go. Great care is needed to ensure that you specify the correct file names for operations like these. If the master file(s) are updated with the wrong transactions (or, for that matter, with the right transactions twice over) it can be very tricky to restore the situation.

Perhaps the most common way that this can occur is getting the date wrong. For example, observe our valiant battle-scarred user, now running the end of month procedure for his integrated accounting package. The system announces something like:

Month end routines: posting sales and purchase details to nominal master file. Please enter month number:

Today is July 11th, so our user counts the months on his fingers and keys in 7 (his lucky number, as it happens). Well, not that lucky, in fact: the system proceeds to feed in to the master file 300 transactions for the first ten days in July, instead of all the transactions for the completed month of June. The finance director wanted the half-yearly figures yesterday; in order to oblige he will now have to reverse all the July transactions (if the system will let him) and then feed in the correct June data before doing the reports.

 Check the manual if you are not sure which file(s) to use

Programs

Every so often a new version of a software package is released. This is usually done to eliminate bugs, sometimes to add new features (especially those boasted by competitors), often both. You will sometimes be offered an upgrade at zero or nominal cost (generally when serious bugs emerge). Even rather more costly upgrades can be worthwhile, but there are two points to watch.

Firstly, you must be certain that files created by the earlier version of the program will still be totally acceptable, presenting no difficulties for the new version. This is sometimes called 'upwards compatibility'. There will sometimes be a special program supplied to convert files in cases where their format is amended.

Check file compatibility carefully before upgrading to new versions of software

Secondly, if you do upgrade your programs, make sure that you don't run the older version by mistake. It is much less likely that your files will be 'downwards compatible': in other words, you could corrupt your data irretrievably if you revert, say, to version 1 having upgraded to version 2 of your package. Therefore:

 Don't leave obsolete versions of software lying about where they could be used by mistake

DISASTER CAUSE NUMBER 18 :   Backup Failure

Most PC users have by now been fairly well indoctrinated: they know that backups are vital to trouble-free computing. Yet failures of the backup process still happen daily. Let's see why.

The risky backup

Some users, however careful they are most of the time, expose their data to risk during the backup process itself. The Disaster-Prone User, determined to change his luck, has just finished copying his files onto his backup disk before starting the next job. At that moment, a thoughtful colleague, bringing him a mug of coffee, trips over one of the mounds of printout surrounding our hero's desk. The coffee is sprayed liberally over his disks. Both the original and backup disks are unreadable from that moment.

This example, too, may be extreme - but any mishap: coffee, heat, magnetism, dust, power surge etc. which can befall a disk can, and occasionally does, simultaneously strike another. Therefore:

 Take at least two backups of any valuable files - on separate media

Which data should be backed up?

My personal view is that the question is rather: are there any files which you can happily afford to lose? Isn't just about all of your data valuable? Certainly any system or program which you run on a regular basis, any system whose output your business or professional practice requires - in fact any system in which you invest your time - comes into the 'valuable' category. You must have ample backups of your data. Don't leave them for the temp or office junior to complete, unless you are fully confident in them: if necessary, make sure they are properly done by doing them yourself.

Rotation and frequency of backups

I would suggest three clearly-numbered backup disks (or *sets* of backup disks) for regular use for each system. They should be rotated so that the next backup will be made onto the least recently used disk. The frequency of backups must be defined: they simply won't get done if the rule is "when time permits". How often depends on how much and how rapidly your data changes. Many users generate enough new data each day to need a backup every afternoon. Each set of backup disks can be labelled e.g. Backup Set 1: Monday disk, Backup Set 1: Tuesday disk, etc. An extra backup is advisable before any major changes (e.g. new release of software, year end, etc.).

 Don't miss a scheduled backup time

The backup log

A log should be kept of what backup was carried out, by whom, onto which disk and exactly when. You can design your own layout, perhaps along the lines of the PC file log suggested on page 62.

 Allow enough time for backups. Carry them out and record the details with care

Checking backup content

Some unfortunate users follow such procedures strictly for years, never once needing to rely on their backup files. Then disaster strikes: a file is lost or corrupted. Only then do they discover that their backup files are unreadable; perhaps they have always been useless.

 Check the actual content of your backups every so often

Remember to take a new set of backups when your programs are upgraded, 'patched' or otherwise amended

All this may well seem like overkill - until you lose your first major file. These essential chores can be streamlined quite a bit, as we shall see in Chapter 8.

Hard disk backups

The same principles apply whether the bulk of your data is on hard disk, floppy disk - or any other medium. The practice may differ. If you are using huge files on your hard disk (more than 300K, say) then floppy disk backups may be impracticable. Similarly, if you are regularly using, and updating, such large numbers of separate data files that you would need more than a few floppies to back them all up, you may need to consider alternative media.

The main options (at the time of writing) are streamer tape, videotape (very slow) and cartridge drives. One or two sources are mentioned in the Appendix.

Insuring against data loss

For some users, it may be worth taking out insurance against data loss and the costs of reconstructing files from scratch. If you can demonstrate that sound backup procedures are in place, the premium payable should be reasonable.

DISASTER CAUSE NUMBER 19 : Backup Location

This is obviously an aspect of backup failure, but is treated as a separate cause of disaster simply to draw attention to it. It is quite incredibly widespread!

It could not be simpler. The Disaster-Prone User keeps his backup disks *in the same box* as his originals. He is asking for trouble, and in due course gets it, when the cleaning lady leaves the box on a radiator while she dusts the windowsills. No data survives.

 Don't keep backups in the same place as your originals

It is not enough to keep backup disks in a separate box. You may have access to a fireproof safe. Remember that a safe which is fine for protecting paper documents may still get far too hot for magnetic media to survive unaffected. The safe should be designed so that the interior gets no hotter than 50 degrees Celsius after one hour's conflagration!

A better, and less dramatic, solution, is simple geographical separation. In other words, keep your backups somewhere else: at the very least in a separate room - but much better to take them to a separate building. Take them home, or if your PC is at home, take them to work, to a friend's - just keep them apart. If both buildings burn down, then give up computing, because someone really has got it in for you. Using this system, you can conduct your regular cyclical backups by taking just one backup disk to the PC at a time; it should be removed again when the backup is complete.

Bear in mind the other aspects of security, if the data in question could be valuable to a competitor or any other thief. With this proviso:

 Always keep backups geographically separate from originals

DISASTER CAUSE NUMBER 20 : PC Dependence

The final, and perhaps most important, cause of PC disaster is an attitude of mind rather than any particular mistake or omission. It is precisely because microcomputers are so reliable that it is easy to obtain a false sense of their infallibility, especially if you have taken sensible precautions to reduce the risk of mishaps. Your systems might run so smoothly and successfully that you come to depend on them totally.

There are numerous horror stories of individuals and companies who have paid dearly for such dependence. Some have gone bankrupt. Their computer systems failed, for a variety of reasons; that alone did not mean curtains. The clincher was the fact that they did not really believe it could happen to them - and consequently had no plans to enable them to carry on without their systems.

Here is a simple four-part plan to help you to avoid becoming a PC disaster story - and to remain a PC success story.

1. Prevent disaster - don't wait for it. Take precautions such as those described in these pages.

2. In case you do run into serious trouble, and are not sure how to solve it: keep a list of helpful 'troubleshooting' contacts by the 'phone. These may include:

> Friends and colleagues
> Your PC supplier
> Your hardware maintenance company (if different)
> Software suppliers (if different)
> User groups or other 'helplines'

3. If being without your PC systems for any length of time could seriously impact your work, arrange in advance for emergency use of another machine in case of major hardware problems. Your maintenance agreement might allow for this or your dealer might even offer such a facility. Otherwise, many users make reciprocal crisis plans with other individuals or organisations.

4. Try to keep your options open with manual alternatives to your PC systems. For example, if you are running your payroll on the PC, keep the up-to-date manual tax and National Insurance tables in the office, just in case. If you are running your busy sales ledger and invoicing system on the PC, keep the old ledger and make sure you still have a working typewriter in the office.

And make sure that someone still knows how to use these alternatives. After all, just because some software house goes out of business the week before your software crashes - there's no reason why you should: hand-typed invoices are still better than none. It may seem strange for a PC book to urge such caution. Of course you never read computer manuals telling you to keep your old paper-based manual systems available as an emergency backup. Computer manufacturers are in business to encourage your faith in the PC, leading to an ever-increasing appetite for hardware and software.

That should be no surprise. The variety of ways in which computers can help individuals and organisations is indeed continuing to expand. Many of these new applications are even hungrier for computer power and storage space. Don't miss out on these opportunities, for they are surely changing the way we live and work. But do take a little time to work out how you or your organisation will fare if somebody pulls the plug.

 Don't become 100% PC-dependent

Chapter Six
Getting Out of Trouble

Before you launch into any dramatic (and potentially dangerous) rescue operations, make absolutely certain that you do actually have a problem. It could just be, for instance, that you have entered a command or a filename incorrectly (check the program manual and/or your records) and have done no real harm.

If there definitely is trouble, is it serious enough to require action? Of course we should be masters, not slaves to our PCs but don't overdo it. If, for instance, a report heading appears two lines further down the page than you want it, don't waste time trying to shift it, unless you are certain that you can do it in a few moments (famous last words!) - live with it. And always keep in mind the American saying:

 If it ain't broke, don't fix it

What kind of problem?

Defining the problem can be surprisingly difficult, especially trying to discover whether software or hardware is to blame. You will normally save yourself time by using the following assumptions:

1. You have made a mistake. (If not you, then someone else with access to your PC.)

2. If you think you have eliminated human error from your inquiries, you may have made a mistake! However, the next most likely cause is a software error.

3. If it is neither you nor your programs at fault, it may be a hardware error.

Before you pack up your PC and cart it off to your dealer or telephone your maintenance company, assuming a hardware failure, make a few simple checks:

1. Is everything securely plugged in, connected and switched on?

2. Have any other obvious mishaps occurred: printer out of paper, snarled up, ribbon exhausted, disk drive door(s) open?

3. Are you using the correct version of the correct program in the correct drive?

4. Did you load it from the correct version of the correct operating system?

5. Are you using the correct data files in the correct directory in the correct drive?

6. Are you trying to write to a protected file or disk?

Before finally blaming your hardware, it is worth checking that your program is still intact; try another copy. If you have used the same copy of a program for a long time, it is quite possible for it to become corrupted. But make sure that you test the same version and, whatever you do:

 Don't use your only backup copy of a program to check out an error; if the program has been wrecked by a hardware fault, the same fault could wreck the backup

Write it Down

Every PC user should keep an Error Log. Write down every problem that crops up. If your ego can stand it, include those silly mistakes which you made and managed to solve yourself: you might help someone else, or be glad of the aide-memoire yourself in six months' time.

Try to record exactly what you were doing when the problem occurred, including all the preceding actions/instructions that you can recall, right down to the last keystroke. Write down any error messages absolutely verbatim, including any obscure codes or other gobbledygook they may include. Your Amstrad manual or your program manual may show you the cause of the problem.

Failing that, your dealer should have technical reference manuals with further messages and additional detail to illuminate the problem(s). They can help only if you can recite chapter and verse.

An Error Log can save you money as well as time; if you do have to call in the maintenance company, their engineer will often be able to diagnose and solve the problem much faster with the aid of a detailed record of software and hardware hiccups.

 Keep a detailed Error Log - and use it to record even simple errors

Don't Panic

If you think your problem is of disastrous proportions, don't panic: it may not be irretrievable. Analyse the situation as calmly and methodically as you can. If you take things slowly you will avoid compounding the problem.

Test one thing at a time

A cardinal rule of fault diagnosis is not to change everything at once. If a car mechanic, suspecting an electrical fault, replaces the battery, coil, spark plugs, distributor and high-tension leads the car may start perfectly - but it will remain a mystery as to which component was faulty, unless they are tested one at a time.

So if, say, your word processing program crashes when you are trying to merge one file with another, you might try a different format for the command, a different copy of the program itself, varying your RAM disk size or using smaller files for the merge operation - but not all four simultaneously, or you may never discover what caused the problem.

When trying to isolate the cause of an unexplained problem, vary only one factor at a time

Don't use your backups!

A common blunder, when a data file seems to have been messed up in some strange way, is to load up the backup copy of the file and try the same procedure again. Chances are, exactly the same problem will afflict the backup copy, too! Backup files are for use only when you are confident that you have identified and resolved the cause of the problem. Don't let the repairperson get hold of your backups, either, until you are satisfied that the fault has been rectified.

Suppose, for example, that your accounting system freezes for no apparent reason in the middle of entering a transaction. From that moment, the master file appears to be inaccessible. If you load up last month's backup files, you risk losing them as well. Even if that is avoided, you may still have to repeat the entry of hundreds of transactions before recovering the status quo.

It could be, on the other hand, that your dealer or software supplier has encountered a similar problem. Knowing exactly how each file is updated during normal operations, they could perhaps advise you on exactly which files, if any, should be restored from backups - and where to go from there.

 Don't just load your backup data files and hope - first identify and solve the problem!

Don't fix anything until you know what's wrong

Once the problem has been properly identified, the solution may be obvious. But if you cannot find out what is really wrong, or work out a suitable remedy, resist the temptation to guess. If you tinker at random you may make irreversible changes, digging yourself into a deeper hole. Use the contact list suggested in the last chapter; the problem might well have been encountered and solved before.

Ask for help if you are at a dead end. Fiddling about at random may make matters worse.

Dealers and Consultants

If you do need to call on professional help, a couple of warnings are in order. Firstly, beware the tendency for hardware suppliers to blame someone else's software, and software houses to be equally convinced that you have a hardware fault. Although this pass-the-buck attitude is not quite so widespread these days, it is still common enough that you need as much evidence as possible about your problem. This is one of the best arguments for 'one-stop' shopping i.e. buying all hardware and software from one reputable dealer. Then there should be no debate about who should provide support when you are out of your depth.

Secondly, beware 'independent' consultants who aren't. They should be able to suggest the simplest, most cost-effective solutions. There are, however, far too many who take commissions from hardware and software suppliers, and by an extraordinary coincidence will steer you towards purchasing the very same hardware and software. While we're on the subject of gravy, much of the ill-founded criticism of the Amstrad PC has emanated from (completely impartial) operators who just happen to have other compatible 'boxes' to shift. These facts are, of course, totally unconnected.

If you do summon professional help, define exactly what you want done. Some unfortunate users have found themselves with unexpected bills for major PC surgery; others have been kept waiting for weeks because they did not discuss the timescale for a diagnostic or repair job.

 Get estimates and set time and cost limits when you seek expert help. Keep a clear written record of any commitments made - on both sides.

RECOVERY METHODS

The Troubleshooting section, towards the back of your Amstrad manual, contains some useful guidance. However, if you have loaded the wrong program by mistake, the manual suggests making a quick getaway, either by holding down Ctrl and pressing Break, or by resetting your PC with another disk. This advice might occasionally be dangerous: as explained earlier, some packages may open files with control records to be updated on exiting, even though you haven't done anything. If your PC system has 'hung up' you may have no alternative, but otherwise:

 Take the proper exit route out of the package.

Mislaid Files/Data

Make sure that you are looking in the right place. Have you specified exactly the correct filename? Are you looking in the right folder/directory? On the right disk? Are you using the right system or program?

Sorted Directories

Remember that you can scan all the filenames in a folder (directory) either at the GEM Desktop (choose icons or text to show the files) or with the DIR command in DOS. It may help to show the filenames in alphabetical order: with GEM, pull down the Arrange Menu and click on Sort by Name, etc. Under DOS, simply type:

DIR | SORT ENTER

to obtain a sorted directory on screen. The | symbol means "take the output from the last command (which was DIR) and feed it into the next command (which is SORT)". If there is more than one 'screenful' of files, typing:

DIR | SORT | MORE ENTER

will wait for you to press a key between 'screenfuls'.

You might wish to bear this sorting facility in mind when you name your files. For example, monthly files called AC0188, AC0288 would appear in order of month in a sorted directory. However, if you had more than one year's files, the sorted sequence would be: AC0188, AC0189, AC0288, AC0289 etc. Therefore:

 If you include dates as part of your filenames, use the reverse date format YYMM or YYMMDD. Then a sorted directory will show your files in date sequence.

If you still cannot remember where your information is located (this should never occur if you are maintaining a log as suggested) you can search to see whether a given string of characters is contained within a file, using the MS-DOS FIND command. For example, typing at the MS-DOS prompt:

FIND "desalination project" C:UAEPROP ENTER

will display any line in the file called UAEPROP on drive C which contains that string. Note that, in this example, the command would not find "Desalination Project".

You can specify more than one file to search, and use the /n option to see where in the file the string occurs, e.g.:

FIND /n "platinum futures" COM001 COM002 COM003 ENTER

will display all occurrences of that phrase, together with their relative line numbers, in each of the three files COM001, COM002 and COM003 on the default drive. But supposing you have no recollection of the likely filename: the missing data could be anywhere. Searching every file on, say, a twenty megabyte hard disk could take a long time. We will see how to automate such a lengthy search in chapter 8.

RAM disk files

You (or your program) might have left the missing file sitting on your RAM disk. Check that possibility before giving up the hunt.

Accidentally Deleted Files

OK, you are quite sure that you have deleted the file you wanted by mistake. GEM and DOS will not help you now. Do not despair: as long as it was a fairly recent error, you still may be able to retrieve the data. A number of cunning little 'utility' programs have been written to carry out all manner of clever tasks - one of which is to 'undelete' files!

Such programs rely on the fact that deleting a disk file does not normally physically destroy the data stored in it, but merely releases the space it took up, making it available again for storage. Provided that no file has physically used that space again (thus overwriting the 'deleted' file's data) you should be able to get it back.

 Before attempting to 'undelete' a file on a floppy disk, take a DISKCOPY of the whole disk. Then if you fail, you're no worse off

One best-selling package of utility programs is the Norton Utilities, available from most dealers; they include a very simple-to-use Quick Unerase, which will restore a recently deleted file. Undelete, from S & S Enterprises will do the same job. The least expensive undelete utilities are available, at nominal cost, from the various user groups (telephone numbers are given in the Appendix). Some utilities (including Norton's) provide more advanced 'undeleting' programs for more awkward cases.

 A utility program to reverse the deletion of files is a good investment

Data lost in RAM

If you have lost RAM data (not in a RAM disk file) e.g. thanks to a program crash, the best bet is to try to work out what went wrong and start again. There are utility programs to help you to retrieve RAM data, but generally you will spend more time tinkering with the utility than you would by starting from scratch.

Readers may be aware of the DOS DEBUG command. I suggest that this is best left to programmers or users with an excess of time on their hands. It is an interesting tool for snooping around your memory or even your program files, but it can swallow up a lot of time - and cause a lot of damage.

 Leave DEBUG to the boffins

How to use Backups

The correct time to use a backup is, of course, when you have established *and* removed the cause of a file's disappearance or destruction. Even then, it is good insurance to take an extra backup of your backup (ideally, though not necessarily, on another PC) before embarking on a restoration procedure.

The MS-DOS RESTORE command (and its companion, the BACKUP command) are supplied only with hard disk models of the Amstrad PC. It could be argued that these commands are too powerful for their own good. The same really applies to the the REPLACE command which is available; you can all too easily overwrite files which were perfectly OK and up-to-date by careless use of this command.

The simplest and safest way to restore files from backups is with the COPY command. For example, if you had lost a word processed file called REPORT66 which should have been on drive B, exit from the program normally, leaving the data disk in B, and put your correct backup disk into drive A. Supposing that you had called the relevant backup version of the file REPORT66.BAK, simply type:

COPY A:REPORT66.BAK B:REPORT66 ENTER

and the file is restored on to drive B. Any edits done since that particular backup was taken will of course have to be repeated; this is where your Backup Log is invaluable, as it will tell you exactly when that backup was made.

Take an extra set of backups before attempting to restore any files from backups

Use a simple COPY command to restore a file from its backup copy

Note that some programs automatically create a .BAK file whenever a file is edited. It is a copy of the same file as it was at the start of the editing session. This is a valuable extra security measure, as well as allowing you to scrap your edits and go back to your original version if you wish. Such .BAK files are, however, placed in the same directory as the newly edited versions, so they are NOT a substitute for proper backups. Be careful not to omit the target filename: if, in the previous example, the command had been:

COPY A:REPORT66.BAK B: ENTER

the restored file on drive B would have kept the .BAK filetype extension. This can be confusing and many word processing programs sensibly refuse to edit a .BAK file.

Turning Back the Calendar

Users who are running systems (especially accounts programs) on a weekly or monthly cycle occasionally find that, having run the period end procedures, a number of transactions appear which should have gone into the previous period. This may not matter (as long as the period end was not the year end also) but if the data is important (e.g. someone's timesheets), if the volume of missed transactions is large, or if you really need precise period end reports, you might need to 'undo' the period end routines so as to admit the stray data into the period to which it relates. In other words, you may occasionally wish to turn back the calendar.

Accounting systems generally will not let you go back a period; if they did, your auditors/accountants, not to mention the taxman, would want to know the reason why. However, the above case is a quite legitimate reason for needing to re-enter an earlier period. As another example, a whole batch of transactions might have been incorrectly entered: say a temporary operator keyed in the month's sales invoices as if they were cash received, so that every entry was posted to the sales account as a debit rather than a credit. This would make nonsense of the accounts for that period, and of the balance sheet. In such circumstances, you could reverse every single erroneous entry, then re-enter them correctly, but it could look rather a mess. You might decide, depending on the volumes involved, that it would be cleaner to go back and start the period afresh.

As long as you have backups of all the relevant files, as they stood immediately after the previous month end procedure, you can replace your current files with these backups and run the whole period again. Three points should be mentioned.

First, keep the 'audit trail' reports showing your aborted period, clearly marked to show why you went back to the start of the period. Second, be sure you really do know which files must be replaced from backups; if you mix files from different periods you can get into deep trouble. Check the manual, and take an extra set of backups before you start the process, just to be on the safe side. Third, bear in mind that you will have to re-enter all the transactions for that period. If they run into hundreds or thousands, you might want to think again; in such cases you should probably have taken interim backups, say at the end of each week. In that case you could 'go back' just a few days rather than a whole month.

As we will see (chapter 8) a restore procedure like this could be automated just as easily as a backup procedure, although (unlike the backup procedure) it should be needed only rarely.

Accidentally Formatted Disks

Until recently, victims of this blunder had no hope: their data was gone for keeps. This was especially disastrous for hard disk users: a few little files is one thing, several megabytes could spell the end of somebody's business. Now that several 'unformat' programs have appeared on the market, there is a fair chance of recovering a good proportion of the original data.

 If you have formatted your hard disk by mistake, do nothing else until you have bought an 'unformat' program

Read/Write Errors

If you ever get an error when reading from or writing to disk, stop what you were doing or the problem may be aggravated. It may be dangerous to take a backup of your data right away (unless you have a second PC available), as a disk drive fault might possibly damage both original and backup.

Simple checks can be performed on a floppy disk drive. Try formatting a blank disk. If that works, insert a disk with obsolete files (which you don't mind risking) and look at its directory: press ESC to tell GEM you have changed disk, or key in DIR ENTER if you are in DOS. If the directory looks normal, with the correct files displayed, the floppy drive is probably OK.

To make sure, the next step is to run a disk diagnostic program. This is an inexpensive utility which can pay for itself in seconds, by alerting you to a disk drive problem before you do any major damage to your data (or your disk drive). Versions are available for floppy and hard disks.

 If you suspect a disk drive fault, run a disk diagnostic program

Corrupted Files and Disks

If the drive itself appears to be healthy, you may have corrupted file(s) on disk. Run the MS-DOS CHKDSK program (supplied on floppy disk 1) by keying, for example:

CHKDSK A:YOURFILE ENTER

with the suspect disk (containing a doubtful file called YOURFILE) in floppy drive A. Remember that CHKDSK is an external command i.e. the file CHKDSK.EXE must be available on the default drive (B or C in this example) to make it work. CHKDSK will give you a report on the disk and for the particular file in question. The entire disk can be checked with:

CHKDSK A: ENTER

CHKDSK can also be used to correct errors but it is safer to use it first for information only, then copy the files which are unaffected one at a time on to another disk. This process is more laborious but safer than trying to DISKCOPY the damaged disk.

 Copy undamaged files to another disk before you attempt any data recovery procedures

Errors in the allocation of space to the files and directories on disk, rather than in the data contained in any particular file, can sometimes be corrected by adding the /F (for Fix) to CHKDSK:

CHKDSK A:/F ENTER

You may find that some of the CHKDSK messages are rather hard to follow, but it will try to correct several different types of error without more ado. The mysterious 'lost cluster' error is fortunately much less common with later versions of MS-DOS, such as are supplied with your Amstrad. CHKDSK cannot, however, help much with recovery of the actual data contained in your files.

Recovery

Having established that a file is damaged or corrupted (as opposed to merely containing incorrect data, perhaps as a result of operator error) the MS-DOS RECOVER command (also supplied on the Amstrad disk 1) may retrieve much of the data. Key in e.g.:

RECOVER A:YOURFILE ENTER

and MS-DOS will recover any data which it can, skipping over 'bad sectors' which are marked so that they will not be used again. After completion, a message such as:

8192 of 10244 bytes recovered

will be displayed. *Always* include a specific filename with the RECOVER command, unless the entire disk has been corrupted. If you issue the command without a filename, it can wipe out perfectly good files.

With the help of a recovery utility program, you might be able to get even closer to complete restoration of your file. Some data corruption is of course irreversible.

Having recovered what you can from a floppy disk, by copying good files and perhaps a recovery of a corrupted file, do not bother trying to reformat and re-use the disk: it really is not worth the risk. And don't just put it back in the disk box; sooner or later, you or somebody else will try to resurrect it.

 Don't try to re-use a floppy disk which has given you trouble. After any recovery procedure, discard the disk

Corrupt Files on Hard Disk

Clearly you cannot throw away a hard disk in such cavalier fashion; you should first conduct any possible salvage operations with COPY, CHKDSK, RECOVER and/or any recovery program you may have available (there are numerous recovery programs designed for hard disks). Having re-created a clean, uncorrupt version of the file it is advisable to mark the corrupted original area(s) on disk by renaming the relevant files rather than deleting them e.g.:

REN SALES0388 BADFILE.001

so as to prevent the system from trying to re-use what might possibly be a damaged zone on the disk. Some hard disk rescue programs will mark bad sectors individually to prevent their re-use. If instead you simply deleted the corrupt file, a further error might occur when the system re-used those sectors on disk. The small wastage of space is worth it.

 Don't just delete corrupted files from a hard disk. Either use a utility which will mark suspect sectors as unusable, or rename the whole file so as to signify that the space is not available

If you have a large number of corrupted files on a hard disk, or keep on getting trouble, you should seek professional help.

Files incorrectly updated

A hazard mentioned earlier involves files which may not be corrupted, but which were not properly updated because of an abnormal exit from the program (user haste, power failure, etc.). There may be vital control totals or other records which, as they are normally amended on exiting the program, are now meaningless.

You may need to restore all relevant files from the latest backup copies, repeating any transactions or changes input since those backups. In some cases, your dealer or software supplier may be able to help with a short cut. This might involve a direct amendment to a control record, or running a special program to re-calculate the missing figures. For this and other disasters, it is always worth asking, just in case someone has passed that way before.

Program Bugs

This is true of program bugs, too. Most of the bugs you might encounter will already have been reported to the software company concerned, who will very often have a 'fix' up their sleeve. In case of serious bugs, you may get a free replacement program by sending in your original disk. Some companies will make a small charge. If the bug is quite easily fixed, they may simply send details of the 'patch' for users to correct the program themselves.

You may have to run the MS-DOS DEBUG program, which enables you to edit binary files directly. As you might guess, you can do all sorts of damage with DEBUG, so follow the instructions supplied as meticulously as possible. Don't experiment unless you really are very experienced in low-level programming.

If you have uncovered a brand new bug, your first task is to convince the software company that you are not completely stupid or incompetent. I would suggest:

1. Take exact and copious notes about the problem.
2. Talk to a technical support person with a genuine knowledge of the product.
3. Don't let them go until you have their name, a commitment as to what they are going to do about it - and when.

Don't be reticent in this situation. You cannot yet expect to buy 100% bug-free software. However, when you do find a serious bug, you have every right to expect it to be resolved as soon as is reasonably possible. Or your money back. If you do obtain a new release of a program, or a fix for any program bugs, remember to take new backups before installation.

Space Problems

Better-behaved programs will warn you when you have (or are about to) run out of space in RAM (main memory). You will then have an opportunity to save your data before it is too late. It may be advisable to reduce the data volume if possible before saving. For example, you may be able to blank out a few redundant spreadsheet cells, or delete a couple of paragraphs: better still, split the file into two chunks. When one chunk is safely saved, you should be able to delete that section from the original file, leaving yourself with a second manageable chunk.

Other programs will not warn you, crashing or hanging up without warning. If you have not been saving your data regularly, there is no easy way to retrieve that data. But you can at least prevent it from happening again. If your program gives you no information as to how much memory space is used/free, you can obtain another inexpensive utility program which will sit beside your application in RAM and tell you on request how much RAM is left. Such programs are also available from user groups (if not your dealer) and have names like RAMFREE.

Disk Space

Suppose that you are trying to save a newly-edited version of a sizeable file on to disk, when your word processing program informs you that there is not enough room on disk. There are then two possibilities:

1. Some word processing programs will allow you to delete one or two unimportant (check carefully!) files from the disk *without* leaving the word processor. This enables you then to save your edited file, thanks to the space you have just released. Problem solved: just take care to leave a bigger space margin next time.

2. On the other hand, some programs will *not* let you delete files until you leave the editor, or worse still, force you to leave the applications program entirely. If you do that without saving, your edits will of course be lost. There are (at least) two ways out of this bind.

RAM-resident software

One method is to run yet another utility program side-by-side with your main application (word processing, say). Since these so-called co-resident programs are actually loaded in part of RAM while you are working, they can be called up from your main program with a key stroke or two. One function of such programs can be to delete files, in this case to get around the space difficulty. Another key stroke or two, and you return to exactly where you left off in your main program. Now you can save your file as usual. Suitable programs can be obtained through your dealer or from a user group; PC Tools and PC Deskmates are two examples.

The second method will work only for floppy disk users (and only with some programs) and requires access to a second machine. Simply take out the data disk from the drive - for once *without* exiting from the program: leave the program exactly where it is. Put the disk into another PC and delete some unwanted files (or copy, then delete, if they are needed). Replace the disk into the first PC and save as usual. Obviously, if another PC is not near to hand, this solution is unlikely to be worthwhile, unless you stand to lose a large amount of work.

 Some RAM-resident software tools can be valuable, not just for functions like diaries and notes, but also to enable you, in an emergency, to carry out disk housekeeping within your application

Fragmented and 'Lost' Disk Space

It is worth noting that all the data in a file is not necessarily stored in one piece. If a disk is fairly full and has been used a good deal, the free space becomes fragmented. Therefore a new file may have to be 'spread' in chunks at different locations on the disk, with pointers indicating where the constituent parts are stored.

The operating system takes care of this, so that there is no need to worry about it, just to be aware that the efficiency of storage and speed of processing files will deteriorate over time. Furthermore, when the size of a file is reduced (e.g. by editing and deleting large parts of it), the space is not always released for re-use. Consequently, the total of all the individual file sizes plus the space available does not always equal the total disk space! This fragmentation and lost space can easily be recovered by copying. A twin floppy user can put the existing disk in drive A, a new blank (but formatted) disk in drive B, and type:

COPY A:*.* B: ENTER

The files will be individually copied to the new disk, with any fragmented or wasted space being sorted out in the process. Note that DISKCOPY will not do this job, as it creates an exact image of the old disk, including any space allocation defects.

Hard disk users can use COPY in a similar way to transfer all the files in one directory to a new, empty directory on the same disk, by, for example:

MD C:\NEWDIR ENTER
(to create a new directory)
COPY C:\OLDDIR*.* C:\NEWDIR ENTER
(to copy the files to the new directory, releasing any wasted space)
DEL C:\OLDDIR*.* ENTER
(to delete all files in the old directory)
RD C:\OLDDIR ENTER
(to remove the old directory)

Periodically, it is well worth using one of the available hard disk reorganisation utility programs. This will free quite a bit of space, rationalise files and improve processing speeds. Some application packages also include their own programs for regular reorganisation of files: especially large, indexed master files which can become very disjointed and inefficient over time.

 Check the free space on your disks regularly, and reorganise them when necessary

Saving to a Write-protected Disk

If you attempt to save a file on to a floppy disk on which the write-protect notch is covered, an error will of course occur, with a message like:

Write protect error writing drive A:
Abort, Retry, Ignore?

If you press A for abort, the system will cancel the writing operation you just requested (e.g. saving a file) but usually no harm is done. If you press I for ignore, the system may get angry and throw you out to the A> prompt. If, however, having checked that you really do want to write to that disk, you remove the sticky label from the disk's write-protect notch, replace the disk and press R for retry, the system should save your file quite happily.

Hardware Failures

If you experience a real hardware failure, there are of course no quick fixes that can get you out of trouble. You must call for professional help as soon as possible. There may be no alternative to new chips, boards, disk controllers or whatever - but make sure you receive an adequate explanation, in language that you, the customer, can understand.

If you have taken sensible precautions, as suggested in the last chapter, you can withstand even the rare event of a major hardware failure. But whatever you do, do not limp on with a faulty system: it can and will get worse.

 Don't try to keep on processing if you think you may have faulty hardware

One last chance for lost data

We dealt earlier in this chapter with the problem of missing data and/or files. Occasionally users may locate the correct file, only to find that a large chunk of the data is no longer there. Or is it? Here is a last straw to clutch at: an end-of-file marker, i.e. control-Z, which can be obtained by pressing function key F6, could have inadvertently been inserted into the middle of the file, instead of (or as well as) at the end, where it belongs. Thus it is just possible that your file only appears to be truncated; the rest of the data could still be there! I have seen this caused in two ways: the first was a program bug which slapped the end of file marker in the wrong place under certain unusual conditions, while the second was an over-hasty user who did not exit from the program in the proper way.

A possible solution

By now, readers may have experimented with RPED or EDLIN, the editor programs provided with your machine. Unfortunately, RPED, the easier program to use, cannot help here, but EDLIN (supplied on your MS-DOS disk, number 1) has an option which enables you to examine a file while ignoring any embedded end-of-file markers. If your suspect file is, say, VITAL.DAT on drive B, you can examine it by typing:

EDLIN B:VITAL.DAT /B ENTER

The '/B' tells the EDLIN program to go past any such markers, so that it will show you any data which might still be lurking in no man's land. If this turns out to be the case, you can use EDLIN itself to remove the offending Control-Z character(s). All the data on file should then become accessible again. Your main manual contains a detailed description of commands available under EDLIN. Let us hope you will never need to try such a long shot.

Chapter Seven
Taking the Pain Out of Printing

Printing can be a real nuisance. When you have begun to get the hang of your PC, having perhaps struggled to achieve mastery over your applications package, you don't relish the idea of going back to the bottom of the learning curve. Printing should be a simple matter of plugging in, pushing a key or two and waiting for the results. As you may have found already, it isn't like that at all.

Many of the niggly problems are about compatibility; most printers are designed as general-purpose machines, not specifically for one computer. Even if they are designed to be fully compatible with your PC, your applications software may well disagree. Some packages can ask more from the printer than it can deliver, while on the other hand some printers have capabilities which the software cannot fully exploit.

The ideal way to avoid most of these problems is to buy your printer in conjunction with your applications packages, to ensure compatibility from the start. But life, and computing, are not usually that simple; in any event, most users will continue to buy further software packages, perhaps for several years after buying their hardware - including the printer.

BUYING A PRINTER

If you have not already bought a printer, how should you go about it? The choice nowadays is bewildering; let's review the main options and their salient features.

IMPACT PRINTERS

Impact printers use the subtle method of bashing out the printed image with physical blows from hammers or little wires. The result is that they are all fairly noisy, even the best ones cannot print especially quickly, and the bits involved with the hammering wear out after a time. Despite all this, most serious users still buy them!

Dot-matrix printers

The dot-matrix printer is the most widespread of all, forming its characters from a grid of dots, each of which is created by a causing a wire to strike the paper through a ribbon. The cheapest models, having fewer wires in the 'print-head' matrix, make fairly crude characters: you can quite easily see the individual dots. At the top end, 24-pin print-heads produce such tiny, cleverly overlapping dots that you have to look very closely to tell that it is matrix printing at all.

Most dot-matrix printers nowadays attempt to give you both types of print: you can switch them between cruder, 'draft' quality for faster printing (up to 500 characters per second or more) and so-called 'near-letter quality' or NLQ, considerably slower but much more pleasing and legible. Even the earlier models, which did not have an NLQ option, can print NLQ output (often in several typestyles) with the help of special utility programs, such as Niceprint.

The Amstrad DMP 3000 and 3160 are inexpensive models claiming respective speeds of 105 and 160 cps in draft mode, and a more sedate 26 and 40 cps in NLQ mode. Their big brother the DMP 4000 has draft/NLQ speeds of 200/50 cps, as well as a wider (15-inch) carriage.

Among the high-quality (24-pin) models in the matrix market are the Epson LQ2500, offering five built-in character fonts, speeds of 270/90 cps and the NEC Pinwriter P9XL, also with several fonts and very respectable speeds of 384/128 cps. The fastest matrix printers can hit 700 cps, but that extra speed adds substantially to the cost.

These printers offer great flexibility. Reasonable graphics output can be achieved by most dot-matrix printers; in their graphics modes they should at least be able to cope with the ASCII graphics characters 128 to 254 (see Appendix 3 of your Amstrad manual), and perhaps manage a reasonable half-tone picture. Some of these machines (e.g. the NEC) can even give colour output of acceptable quality by means of a multi-coloured ribbon.

The NLQ output of a good matrix printer is of such quality as to be satisfactory for almost all purposes. Usually proportionally spaced (so that, as with typeset material, thin letters like l take less room than fat ones like w) it is certainly more than adequate for business correspondence, and now rivals the quality of some of the cheaper daisywheel printers.

Daisywheel printers

These printers take their name from their printwheels which vaguely resemble daisies, carrying fully-formed letters at the end of each 'petal'. The daisywheel is rotated until the required character is uppermost, in position to be struck against the ribbon by a hammer.

This process is necessarily slow and noisy, but gives an outstanding quality of print. Good daisywheel printout still has the edge over the best dot-matrix print, but the gap is now very small. Given that the daisywheel really is too noisy for extended use without an acoustic hood, which significantly boosts its price, it is easy to see why daisywheel sales are being squeezed. All daisywheel printers offer several character pitches and most of them can also handle proportional spacing. There is usually a wide range of daisywheels available, giving a greater variety of fonts than most matrix printers.

Top speed for daisywheels means not much more than 90 cps, with models like the Qume sprint 90. Near the bottom end in speed and price terms is the pedestrian Brother HR10, which races up to a maximum of 12 cps. There are clearly trade-offs between print quality, speed and noise level. The Brother Twinwriter actually manages to combine a 40 cps daisywheel with a 160 cps draft dot-matrix mode in one printer. There is a distinct trend, however, away from impact printers altogether.

NON-IMPACT PRINTERS

Thermal printers

Thermal printers have generally been regarded as the poor relation of the entire printing family. They produced unappealing, smudgy output and required special paper to work at all. This technology is somewhat improved of late (several manufacturers, including IBM, now have thermal printers of quite good quality in their range. Thermal printers are widely used where a compact mechanism is needed: printing calculators, portable printers and data logging terminals all use thermal mechanisms. It is also used in good, but pricey, colour printers; though not perfect, it will remain the first choice for some users who need full colour print, until laser or similar technology delivers cost-effective colour.

Ink-jet printers

These form characters from individual dots, like dot-matrix printers. In place of the wires used by the dot-matrix printer, the ink-jet has a grid of minute ink guns firing at the paper.

This process was as erratic as it sounds; until recently, ink-jet quality and reliability were poor. The latest models, however, have changed the whole picture. The Epson SQ2500, for instance, seems to be outstandingly reliable, offers five built-in fonts and produces excellent quality print at a respectable 180 cps (or 540 cps in draft mode!). Although they are relatively expensive, such printers now frequently outperform their dot-matrix equivalents. They have the further major advantage of being virtually silent in operation. One or two very compact portable printers use ink-jet technology e.g. the Diconix 150, one of the few viable printers that really will fit into a briefcase.

Laser printers

If you still haven't blown your budget, laser printers are better still. In just a few years, prices have plummetted; early laser printers were large engines costing half a million pounds or more, suitable only for the biggest computer installations. Now several desktop models are available for less than £2000.

A good laser printer, used with care, will yield even better quality than a daisywheel, but very much faster. Furthermore, it is more flexible than any other printer. Most models have several character fonts (sometimes dozens) built-in as standard; others can be loaded as required, possibly direct from your applications program. The size of letters can usually be varied, with the option of using several typefaces within a document (for different levels of heading, captions, etc.). In addition, graphics output can be produced and integrated with text or other data if required.

This enables so-called *desktop publishing* of, for example, illustrated brochures, newsletters, reports incorporating graphs and charts, and so on. Businesses can print invoices, orders, payslips, etc. without the need for specially-printed stationery: the form itself, including ruled lines, boxes and logos, can be printed together with the facts and figures it contains. The only limiting factor is usually the applications package, which has to be able to generate such sophisticated output, and send it to the printer in the right format. Several programs are strong in this area, allowing direct graphics output to laser printers.

The average laser printer is so fast that several PC users can easily share one on a network (stand-alone PCs can also share using a special device) without normally noticing any delay in printing. Speeds of 10 pages per minute are not unusual, although heavy use of graphics can reduce some laser printers to a snail's pace.

Laser print quality is usually measured in terms of dots per inch. At a resolution of 300 dots per inch (the norm for many lasers) individual dots become almost invisible, unless you peer very closely at the letters (look at this page, for example: the resolution is 300 dpi). Epson's GQ-3500 is a low-cost example of a 300 dpi printer, with several standard and numerous optional fonts, which are held on credit-card sized devices. These are simply plugged into special slots on the printer.

The next generation of printers is pushing the resolution as high as 600 dpi and beyond, where the output begins to rival traditional typesetting quality. Do not argue this point with professional typesetters; their machines typically scan over 1000 lines to the inch. Most ordinary folk, however, need a magnifying glass to detect any 'stepping' effect in the letters printed by, say, the Agfa P400 (which actually uses LED rather than laser technology). It can print up to 18 pages per minute at a resolution of 406 dpi but is considerably more costly than a basic laser printer. AM Varityper and Panasonic are two of the companies who have launched 600 dpi laser printers, but the prices are well into five figures - way beyond most Amstrad users' budgets.

SELECTION CRITERIA

Individual circumstances will sometimes dictate a clear printer choice, but the buyer is often torn between all the technologies and variations on offer. The following criteria should help you decide:

Cost

For many users, this has to be the overriding criterion. You can obtain a PC printer (just) for less than £100, and you can also fork out several thousand. Set a budget, then decide your essential printer features, followed by the desirable ones. Surveying the market, you will either be pleasantly surprised, or have to be more ruthless in defining absolute essentials.

 Remember to include any necessary interfaces and cables in your costings, and make an allowance for 'consumables' costs: ribbons, daisy-wheels, ink or toner cartridges, etc.

Compatibility

Will the printer behave properly with your PC and with your applications programs, now and in the future? You may have no idea as to which programs you will be using in a year's time, but if you think it is quite likely that you will be using, say, Lotus 1-2-3 or SuperCalc4, check that the printer can handle the output.

Conversely, when your printer is installed, don't buy any software package before checking that it will work correctly and happily with your printer. Study the user manual: it will often list a whole host of printers in an appendix. If your printer (check the exact model) is listed as being supported, you should be OK.

The package will often include special files called printer drivers. These, when properly set up, tell the program what sort of data and control codes to send to your printer, depending on the output required. Writing or editing your own drivers is not recommended, so if your printer does not feature, be very cautious.

Beware claims that printers are IBM-compatible or Epson-compatible. Both companies sell many different printer models, and few manufacturers agree on a definition of 'compatible'. The printer may have all the features of, say, the Epson LQ1000 but that does not ensure that your programs will always be able to exploit those features.

Your dealer may be able to reassure you, but if in doubt, the only real test is to run the program in question on a PC like yours with the printer in question. Try to get them on approval; failing that, take your software to the dealer's showroom/offices and ask to try it there. If your local dealer can't or won't let you, find one who will. Of course the dealer's profit on a printer does not allow for hours of testing and evaluation - but then one day you (or someone you point in their direction) might buy a much bigger system from them... Do not be reluctant to make any purchase conditional upon compatibility with your system; no reasonable dealer should ever refuse such an agreement. The painless way to enforce it is:

 Don't part with your money until you are satisfied that the printer (or software package) is compatible with your system. Test, if possible, the printer/ software/PC combination before you buy

Output quality

A couple of years ago, it was simple: if you wanted high quality, you chose a good daisywheel printer. Now, with the technological advances outlined above, the choice for top-quality output is far less clear-cut. A top-quality dot-matrix or ink-jet, as mentioned, can almost match daisywheel output, with the added advantages of graphics capabilities, even including reasonable half-tones from some models. One or two top-range dot-matrix printers can (like daisywheels) use carbon ribbons, giving an excellent, dense image. The highest quality available now is undoubtedly achieved by the latest laser printers. With appropriate software, they can not only provide a variety of typefaces and point sizes but also integrate text and graphics within a single printed page. If presentation is critically important to you and you can justify (and afford!) the cost, choose a laser (or LED) printer.

Speed

First-time buyers are often misled by the apparent speed of printers, when demonstrated in the showroom. Compared, perhaps, to many users' two-fingered typing efforts, any printer seems to be rattling along at a decent lick, even a 15 cps daisywheel. Hook the same printer up to the PC back in the office, tell it to print a lengthy report and you will see how slow that really is: it could take a couple of hours!

Estimating print volumes

Many users tend to underestimate the volume of printing that they will require, concluding that speed is not an issue. It usually is. Estimate the number of pages you think you might need to print on a busy day and multiply by a generous factor: 3 or 4, say, to allow for underestimation and growth. Suppose that gives a total of a modest 250 pages. Allowing 2000 characters per page, your printer must deliver up to half a million characters of output per day!

The speeds claimed by manufacturers should not be taken as gospel. The cps figures are usually maximum speeds, obtained 'on the burst' in ideal circumstances. Similarly, the pages per minute quoted by laser manufacturers are likely to be for repetitive work, with few font changes and no graphics. To be safe, halve the claimed speed of the printer in question: let's say it is a '25 cps' daisywheel model. At this (more likely) average speed of 12.5 cps, this printer would have to beaver away for 500,000/12.5 = 40,000 seconds, i.e. over 10 hours non-stop! Conclusion: this printer alone simply could not cope with such a workload; even a fast dot-matrix would be kept fairly busy. More importantly, the user(s) concerned would probably be spending a great deal of their time waiting for printout.

 Make a generous estimate of your printer's workload and a conservative estimate of its speed. If in doubt, opt for a faster model

Noise

Impact printers are loud, daisywheels especially so. Whether this is a problem depends on your tolerance level, and that of your colleagues. Your volume calculations (see above) are relevant; most people can stand some clattering every half hour or so, but not continuously. You can entomb your printer in an acoustic hood, complete with mod cons such as a cooling fan (even those can be annoying!) but the extra cash (several hundred pounds) would probably be better spent, without compromising print quality, on one of the quieter printers which are now available.

Flexibility

Switching from high-speed, draft printing to lower-speed quality printing is indispensible to many users. Some people need a specific range of typefaces, sizes or pitches available. Others have to be able to switch rapidly to foreign character sets, accents, mathematical and scientific symbols, and so forth. Now that the software is available, a growing proportion of PC owners are expecting their printers to be able to handle text and graphics with equal agility, even on the same page. Printing graphs and charts is now common-place; more specialist applications include reproduction of photographs and generation of bar codes.

Paper options

If you think you might, at some point in the future, want to print out charts, spreadsheets or other documents on wider paper than usual, it could be worth paying the extra now for a wider carriage model. Some narrow (8.5 inch) carriages will not even take a standard envelope. There are two main methods of feeding paper through your PC. *Friction* is used, just like a typewriter, normally to feed single sheets; although continuous stationery can be fed by friction, it will sooner or later snarl up. For all but the lightest printing loads, a *tractor feed* is advisable. This device grips the paper with little cogs which engage on sprocket holes at the edges of the paper.

 Even for modest printing needs, a tractor feed will save time by minimising screwed up or misaligned print

You can obtain good quality 'micro-perforated' stationery for a tractor feed. When the sheets are separated, and the sprocket hole strips at the sides are torn off, the perforations are so small as to be almost invisible, and you are left with a normal-looking sheet of the required size. The paper length does not have to equate to an exact number of half-inch sprocket holes, so you can easily use, for example, micro-perforated A4. Such paper can of course be pre-printed with your letterhead, logo or form design. An alternative is continuous computer paper with headed notepaper stuck on with a special peel-off gum (it stays on the carrier sheet rather than your headed paper) but this can give feeding problems.

Cut sheet feeders will typically hold up to 100 sheets of A4, feeding single sheets at the touch of a button or (much better) under software control. These used to be rather temperamental devices, but reliability is now much improved. If you rarely need to switch from A4 printout, and have no need for continuous stationery (e.g. for payroll or accounting reports), a sheet feeder will save you hours every month. Laser printers have their own built-in sheet feeders in the form of a photocopier-style paper cassette, which can be loaded with, say, 250 sheets. A4 is the normal size, though some models go up to A3.

 A cut sheet feeder attached to your printer could save you a few seconds for every page you print

How many copies?

PC users often need more than one copy of printed output. File copies of correspondence must be kept, reports must be circulated to colleagues or other parties, copies of accounting reports, payslips etc. must be retained for reference, audit, statutory and security purposes. Carbon copies are fiddly but you can produce one carbon with a dot matrix printer, perhaps two with a daisywheel (the force of the impression may be adjustable). Special 2-, 3- or 4-part stationery is a quicker and cleaner way of obtaining copies; such stationery can also be pre-printed to produce separate documents at a single printing e.g. top copy: dispatch note, second copy: invoice etc. The best type to buy is 'carbonless', saving time and mess when separating copies.

Non-impact printers can produce copies only by repeated printing of documents. However, their superior speed (especially in the case of laser printers) enables them to run off two or three 'top copies', often in the time it takes an impact printer to print once with a not-too-presentable carbon copy.

Another common requirement, particularly for those sending out extensive mailings, is the ability to print envelopes and/or labels. Envelope feeders are an increasingly widespread optional extra; continuous envelopes can also be obtained. Labels of various sizes can be bought as continuous stationery or on single A4 sheets. Several word processing programs now have mailing options; their features include label-printing routines. Labels sometimes lift off their continuous backing and stick themselves to the printer platen. This problem is usually cured by better-quality labels; one or two printers actually offer a 'straight-through' vertical label feed method to avoid bending labels round the platen: worth considering, perhaps, for heavy direct mail users. The Facit B-Line printer, for example, has four different paper paths - for labels, thicker paper, multi-part forms, etc.

Convenience

Other convenience factors include ease of use, and the way in which various settings can be changed. Some of these changes will be effected on the printer itself, others through software control. Is it quick and easy to:

change typefaces? change pitch?
switch to/from proportional spacing?
load paper? change paper size/type? change ribbons?

It is a nuisance to have to watch a printer throughout its operation; it should be possible to start a print run and get on with another task while the printer completes the job. However, even the best-behaved printers need an occasional check:

 Don't leave a printer completely unattended: paper snarl-ups or other mishaps can cause more damage if not quickly rectified

Reliability

It is not easy to get hard facts about printer reliability. Manufacturers often publish MTBF (mean time between failures) figures in their specifications (usually at least two or three thousand hours). Do not rely on these too far, though, and note that they vary with the maker's assumptions on printing activity and density. Ask around as much as you can for confirmation, but make due allowance as usual for (a) dealers, 'consultants' and even user groups, who may be selling particular printers, and (b) users themselves, who may sing the praises of any machine they use to confirm the wisdom of their purchases.

Making your choice

When choosing from your shortlisted printers, beware of manufacturers' comparison charts, with solid columns of ticks showing that the advertised printer has every feature mentioned while the competition is sadly lacking. You should determine your own list of essential and desirable features, which can easily be quite different from the printer vendor's.

It is also a mistake to equate high cost with high quality. Some expensive printers are excellent; others are just overpriced. One example from the author's experience is a Juki daisywheel: this well-engineered machine has been producing good quality print almost every day for several years, without a single breakdown. Despite its noise level and poor speed, it is an outstanding printer for the price.

Users sometimes ask whether second-hand printers are a good buy. Obviously it depends, but as with a car it is important to establish the reason for sale. Bankrupt stock does often provide bargains, but why should a going concern sell a printer? It just might be getting a bit temperamental. You are probably more likely to get a good second-hand computer than a printer, as there is simply less mechanical wear and tear.

 Don't consider a second-hand printer (or other equipment) without a very thorough test

CONNECTING YOUR PRINTER TO YOUR PC

If care has been taken to check the compatibility of the printer with your PC, as well as that of the software, connecting it up should be straightforward. Some points to remember:

Check whether the printer interface (jargon for the method by which your PC communicates with your printer) is parallel (the most common version is called Centronics) or serial. With a serial interface, data is sent to the printer one bit at a time, whereas a parallel interface has (at least) eight parallel wires, along which the eight bits of a byte (representing one character) can be transmitted simultaneously. In practice, it matters little which type of interface your printer uses, but if for any reason you wanted the printer located at a distance from the PC, parallel transmission might cause problems, as the bits can get 'out of step' over a longer distance.

Ensure that the printer cable is plugged into the correct socket at the back of your Amstrad. Most printers work through the parallel socket (labelled 'parallel printer', although serial printers can be connected to the socket marked 'serial interface'. Use the minimum of force to insert or remove plugs - and if the plugs have securing screws, do not tighten them too much. Once your printer is connected, leave it alone. Repeated removal and reinsertion of cable plugs is a good way of bending a pin or two.

Some users have two printers: a dot-matrix and a daisywheel is a common combination. Others share a printer between more than one PC (but are not using a network). If you're in either category, buy a special printer switch. It will save time and reduce the chance of damaging plugs or sockets. If you happen to have one parallel and one serial printer, never have them both plugged in to your PC at once. This can cause major damage to your PC's circuit boards.

 Limit parallel printer cables to, say, 5 metres

Don't use too much force when plugging/unplugging cables between your PC and your printer

If you want to switch your PC between printers, or your printer between PCs, install a switch designed for the task

Opinions differ as to whether you should switch on peripherals such as printers before or after your PC. Experience suggests, however, that the act of switching on or off a power-hungry device like a printer can cause a power surge. Therefore:

 Switch the power on for your printer before you switch on your computer; conversely, switch the printer power off after switching off your computer

Testing

Most printers have a built-in self-test procedure. This is usually started by keeping one of the printer's control buttons depressed while you switch on the power (check the printer manual first). The output consists of continuous, repeated printing of the entire character set. You might be forgiven for thinking that was the end of the story. No, the fun is just beginning.

GETTING THE OUTPUT YOU WANT

For some day-to-day applications, you may not be too fussy about getting perfect printouts, as long as you have some kind of printed record. However, any document which is intended to be sent out or circulated should be as well-presented as possible, as otherwise it reflects on the sender and the organisation. Anyway, minor print problems can become major annoyances unless they are resolved.

The placing of output on the page may depend on:

The left and right margins, as seen by the program
The left/right positioning of the paper in the printer
The top and bottom margins, as seen by your program
The vertical positioning of paper in the printer
The page length, as seen by the program
The page length, as seen by the printer

There will be a standard, or default, left and right margin set by your program. Accounts reports may always leave, say, a left margin of 2 characters before starting to print, while a word processing program might leave 8. Distinguish, when word processing, the pre-set print margin (sometimes called the offset) from the lefthand margin in the document itself (and on screen). Both figures are usually adjustable; to calculate how far the printer will move across the page before actually printing, you must add these two margins together. The *right*hand margin is preset by the program (for word processing, at perhaps column 70) and together the two margins determine the number of characters on a line. The feed mechanism on your printer should be set up so that the print is correctly positioned; if this necessitates having the paper at the very end of the platen, the margins should be adjusted within the program. Paper feeding problems are likely if the paper is not fairly central.

Similarly, the top and bottom margins, and the page length, are automatically set by your program. With word processing programs you can adjust these, but not always with other packages. Most spreadsheets will let you specify the paper length, but many accounts programs simply assume a standard paper length, say 11 inches. The manual should give the details.

To complicate matters, the printer has its own idea of how long a sheet of paper is. This is usually set by a combination of tiny 'DIP switches', inside or at the back of the printer. They can be switched, when the printer power is off, with a delicate prod from an electrical screwdriver. Thus conflicts can arise between the form length setting in the printer and in the software. Usually, the software overrides the hardware but if the printer ejects a page before it has finished printing, there may be an incorrectly set DIP switch.

Assuming the standard six lines per inch (see below for variations) an 11 inch sheet is 66 lines long, an A4 sheet 70. Remember, too, that these are not print lines: they include top and bottom margins. These are also given default settings by your program. The draft manuscript for this book, for example, was printed on A4 with a top margin of 3 lines, 59 print lines and a bottom margin of 8 lines. Some programs, e.g. payrolls, force you to buy special printed stationery (a) because they do not give the option to print headings, assuming that they will be on the stationery, and (b) because they can only print on one, pre-set form length. Form length, and other printer settings, can be altered by your sending special control codes to the printer. A number of these are discussed below but on the whole, they should be avoided if there is an alternative method: you are in danger of becoming a programmer and you cannot afford the time!

Try to ensure that all margin and page length settings are consistent between your software and your printer

Another DIP switch may need to be set before you can use continuous stationery; if this is not done the printer may have to be reset before each page, which rather defeats the object! Cut sheet feeders usually need the same setting, as if you were using continuous paper.

The right characters

Having got the print where they want it on the page, some users find that they cannot get all the characters they want to print. Your Amstrad PC is initially set up to use the UK character set, plus the ASCII graphics characters mentioned above. So when you press the £ key (shift 3), a £ sign appears on screen (if it doesn't, you are probably using software which has altered the keyboard setup). One way of switching back to UK characters is to enter the KEYBUK command at the DOS prompt (KEYBUK.EXE is a command file delivered on your floppy disk number 1). Better still, ensure that there is a KEYBUK command in the AUTOEXEC batch file as described in Chapter 8.

The printer must also be set up for the UK character set; again, this usually entails setting a combination of DIP switches on the printer itself. If you happen to be using an Amstrad DMP printer, you should set it for the 'European IBM' character set; many printers have a specific UK setting. If you still have trouble:
1) Did you switch off the printer before changing the DIP switch settings? Apart from the danger (to you and the printer) of leaving the power on, the changes will not be recognised anyway by the printer unless it is switched off and powered back up under the new settings.
2) Are you using a daisywheel, golfball, font cartridge or other removable print element? It may not be a UK version. The first time I ever set up a customer's daisywheel printer, I struggled for some time to get it to print £ signs on their reports. Eventually I discovered that the printer had been delivered with a US daisywheel; there wasn't a £ sign to print!

If you want to use another character set: French, for example, a method of switching your PC keyboard under MS-DOS is to use the KEYBFR command. This may not be supplied with your Amstrad PC, but is a readily available MS-DOS command, along with equivalents for other European languages. If your application will run under DOS Plus, another method of setting the keyboard to a foreign character set is described in the Amstrad manual. This procedure includes an option to describe your printer to the program but, either way, you will probably have to change DIP switches.

Accents

Printing accents over characters may be achieved in several ways, depending on your hardware and software. The problem has two facets: getting the accent on screen, and getting it on paper.

1) If you have switched to the French keyboard, for example, pressing the number 2 on the top row of the keyboard will give you an é on screen. Otherwise, hold down the ALT key, tap out the number 130 on the numeric keypad, release ALT and voilà (à is 0 on the 'French' keyboard, or ALT 133!). A third method, used by some word processing packages, is to type a normal e, insert a 'backspace' command (your word processing manual shows you how) and then type the accent itself (the character used depends on your printer).

2) The way you actually show the character on screen depends of course on what your printer can do with it. If it can print the ASCII graphics characters 128 to 254, no problem - as long as it is set to the correct mode to do this. If it is, say, a daisywheel printer, ALT 130 will probably not mean a thing to it: you need a French printwheel (quite easy to obtain) and the correct dipswitch settings. Even then, some characters, e.g. vowels with a circumflex accent, may still require a backspace embedded in your word processed text, in order to get the accent above the letter.

All this can be simplified by creating different versions of your printer drivers. These files are consulted when printing commences in order to 'translate' codes sent from the computer into the desired codes which the printer will understand. Unless you are an experienced user, this job should be left to your dealer.

It may be that the installation procedure for, say, a word processing package will automatically modify the printer drivers to give the output required. Unfortunately, you cannot always rely on this.

An easy way to test the printing of any complete character set is to create a file (using either your word processor, RPED (the editor supplied with your Amstrad PC) or EDLIN (the MS-DOS editor)). Simply include every character on the keyboard, noting the sequence in which you insert them. Save the file and then print it; you will quickly spot any discrepancies between the characters you keyed in and those which your printer delivered. You can of course extend the test to include graphics characters by keying in ALT combinations as described above.

 Test your printer's character set by editing and printing a simple character set file

The right typeface

Changing typefaces may be an option available within your word processing program. That may in turn necessitate the installation of several separate print drivers: one for each typeface available. Otherwise, there will often be a switch on the printer itself to change from draft to letter quality and back again. But to get all the other possible fonts: different typestyles as well as condensed, enlarged, etc. the printer has to be sent the correct control codes. (Daisywheel printers are of course exceptions: swopping the printwheel may be all you need to do.)

Let us take an example: most Epson printers can output condensed print; this is useful, for example, if you want to print a fair-sized spreadsheet without sticking pieces of paper together (see also 'Fancy stuff' below). Equally, you might want enlarged mode sometimes - even italics. However, there are no switches to invoke condensed or other printing modes, and many word processing programs are not yet clever enough to manage it. For this, the correct control codes must be sent to the printer. How is this done? Printer manuals are not too helpful, expecting you to dash off a quick BASIC program to be run whenever you want to change typeface.

The program sends the codes to change the printer status - then you carry on printing. In fact, this is easier than it might sound: you can write a series of one-liners, or combine them into a single printer control program. Always check that the printer is switched on and on-line before sending control codes. Then, for example, executing the following BASIC-2 statement:

LPRINT CHR$(15);

will switch on condensed print for most Epson printers. Print will stay compressed until the statement:

LPRINT CHR$(18);

or some equivalent is executed, whereupon subsequent print reverts to normal size. Users inclined to programming can control all their printer's functions with the aid of a BASIC-2 program. There is another way of achieving the same result, using the MS-DOS ECHO command in a batch file. This is simply a file containing one or more MS-DOS commands. Simply typing the name of the batch file will cause execution of all the commands within it. As with BASIC-2, you can write one-liners, or if you are really keen build an all-singing menu-driven interactive batch file to offer every print option. The following command, contained in a single line batch file:

ECHO ^O > PRN

(the ^ symbol appears when you press Ctrl; say ECHO ^O > AUX if you have a serial printer) will set compressed print on, while a similar file containing just:

ECHO ^S > PRN

will turn it off again. These two batch files could be called, say, COND.BAT and UNCOND.BAT. Simply keying in COND or UNCOND at the DOS prompt would then have the desired effect, as long as those little files were available to DOS. If you preferred the previous method, your BASIC-2 programs could equally be called COND.BAS and UNCOND.BAS.

Some word processing programs will allow you to run a program or execute a batch file without leaving the word processing program itself. This obviously saves time, enabling you rapidly to run COND.BAT or some other file immediately prior to printing, if you wanted condensed output. You will probably find it easier to use batch files than BASIC-2 programs in this respect. Similar code sequences may be required to invoke expanded, italic and other scripts where available. Your printer may have several typeface options available.

Underlining

Obtaining underlined print is nearly always easier: the majority of word processing programs now include this feature at the very least, with print drivers to ensure that the correct codes are sent to switch it on and off. If the text which you underline via your word processing program does not print correctly, check again that you have the correct print driver - not only available, but actually installed. You may have to send the correct codes yourself for several other print functions, if your word processing program does not offer them. Among the most important ones are:

Emphasised or Double-Strike modes :
These increase the print density, usually by printing each character twice, the second time after a fractional vertical or horizontal movement. One of these modes will usually be easily invoked by emboldening text within a document.

Line spacing :
Usually 6 lines per inch; can be set e.g. to 8 lpi, or other values enabling all sorts of fancy graphics output.

Character pitch :
With some printers, this needs to be reset when changing typeface: there may be a switch on the printer itself - most typefaces use 10 or 12 characters per inch, but 15 is not uncommon and e.g. Epson condensed works out at 17.6 cpi.

Proportional spacing :
Certain typefaces e.g. a good NLQ matrix font, are proportionally spaced. This feature may be automatically switched on by selecting that typeface, but sometimes you must flip a switch, or even send a

control code sequence to the printer. A proportional typeface printed without proportional spacing looks dreadful! Some printers throw a fit when you use a proportional typeface together with a lot of underlining, emboldening or - worst of all - accents. There is always a solution but you might save time if you can bear to use a non-proportional typeface in such cases. One further thought:

 Don't reset (warmstart) your PC when you have issued printer control sequences, as they will all be lost; the printer will return to its normal starting status

Fancy stuff

There are plenty of clever programs on the market designed to enhance printer performance. Some inexpensive utilities (ultra-low-cost versions e.g. PC-Print, Set-Prtr are available from user groups) will switch your printer between different modes and typefaces, saving you the trouble of writing and testing your own routines. Other programs enable even the earlier matrix printer models to produce not only presentable NLQ print, but also numerous different typefaces. Tasprint, for example, offers no less than 24 fonts. Others have names like Niceprint, Imageprint, etc.

You can use many printers to create signs with giant letters, with the help of programs like Banner, Banner Builder, Sign, Blkprtr; none of these is expensive. Matrix printer users may find that even condensed printing still does not enable them to print, say, the whole of their spreadsheet across the page. Help is at hand: programs like Sideways, Sideline and Sideways Print will turn the output on its side, printing any required number of columns along the printout. A brilliantly simple solution to a genuine problem, such programs have deservedly sold well.

QUICK PRINTING

There are several shortcuts to speed up printing, especially at times when you do not need perfect output. Holding down the Shift key and pressing PrtSc will give you an immediate printout of the current screen display. This is a useful way of quick printing, e.g. to record a system configuration screen, or to get a rough idea of how a document will look on paper before you complete it.

Any graphics characters on screen, including ruled boxes and symbols, will only be printed correctly if (a) your printer can handle them, and (b) you have issued the GRAPHICS command. If your printer *can* handle graphics output, first ensure that the GRAPHICS.EXE file is available to MS-DOS (it is supplied on the MS-DOS disk 1) then simply type:

GRAPHICS ENTER

This will set up, for example, the Amstrad DMP3000 printer (or the IBM PC Graphics Printer or any compatible model) ready for output of a screen display by pressing Shift and PrtSc. Another common use of PrtSc is to record disk directories as displayed on screen. You may prefer to use the DOS command:

DIR > PRN ENTER
(or DIR > AUX ENTER if you have a serial printer)

which will send the directory straight to the printer. Make sure the 'arrow' of the > symbol is pointing the right way, i.e. towards the printer device name, PRN or LPT1. Alternatively:

DIR | SORT > PRN ENTER

will print out an alphabetically sorted directory. This command can be amended to provide, if preferred, directories sorted by filetype, by size or by date. Simply sort the directory from character positions 10, 14 or 22 respectively. Thus:

DIR | SORT / + 14 > PRN ENTER

will print out the default directory, sorted by filesize. Make sure, however, that there is some space on the default disk for the SORT command to place the temporary file created in the sorting process; it will not work on a write-protected disk for this reason.

GEM lovers may remember that sorting directories is simple at the GEM Desktop; the advantage of the above DOS commands is the immediate printing. Some users keep track of files by switching to condensed print, then printing a compact directory to slot carefully into the appropriate disk envelope.

Turning your printer into a typewriter

Holding down Ctrl while you press PrtSc will cause any subsequent keyboard input (and screen output) to be echoed, character by character, to the printer. Repeat the process to reverse it. A similar result is obtained by typing:

COPY CON: PRN ENTER

To switch off this 'typewriter', press function key F6, then ENTER. This offers yet another way of rapid listing of directories or files. The DOS TYPE command will list any file on to the screen. If strange characters and bleeps crop up, it may be a program or some other file not intended for straightforward listing. If the output is OK, you can again obtain hardcopy by directing it to the printer:

TYPE WIDGETS.DOC > PRN

If you try TYPEing word processed documents instead of printing them from within the word processing program, you may find some strange characters occurring. These will be due to the method employed by the program to store the file. Furthermore, tab characters may not be expanded to the required number of spaces. You can obtain a utility program to fiddle about converting these awkward characters but it really will not be worth the trouble and you could do some damage. Instead, print those files from within the word processing program; you can still use TYPE as a quick check on the contents of a file.

PRINTING BOTTLENECKS

Printing remains about the slowest operation ever carried out by a PC user. Even when you have your printer perfectly configured, can easily switch between modes and typefaces and are churning out perfect output, time still drags if you have any but the lightest printing load. There are a few ways of reducing, if not actually eliminating, the printing bottleneck:

1) Seriously question the volume of print you are generating: some users tend to print anything and everything. If you have made one or two amendments to a long document, you may only need to reprint a page or two: not the whole thing. Some accounts packages

can produce giant reports: do you need to print, say, a complete year-to-date transaction or master ledger listing every week? Will you, seriously, use that information?

2) Install (or enlarge) a print buffer: this device is simply a chunk of extra storage, fitted to your printer rather than your PC. The next load of data to be printed is shunted into this storage area until the printer has finished printing the previous load. The time saving comes when the computer can send the last load of data to be printed into the buffer; then the PC itself is freed for the next job. Most printers have a buffer these days, but it may not hold much: anything less than about 2K (about a pageful of print) is not much help. With a decent sized buffer installed (say at least 8K - they can go up to 40K or more) the PC will be rapidly released when printing all but the largest documents.

3) Use a print spooler: this software alternative to a printer hardware buffer can be a cheaper solution. If you are running a GEM application the GEM Print Spooler may be available to it (see the Amstrad manual for details). If you are usually running MS-DOS applications, there are several compatible, inexpensive spooler programs available. They send your print output to an intermediate file, usually in main memory (a much faster process than printing) thus freeing the PC itself, while printing carries on, sending data from RAM to printer. Clearly, you need to ensure that there is enough memory available before this will work. All mini-and mainframe computer systems, incidentally, use some method of print spooling, though output is normally routed to disk or tape.

4) Try background printing: another way of printing while you use your PC for the next task is provided by the DOS PRINT command. This enables you build a list of files to be printed from disk - a print queue - which DOS then proceeds to print one by one while you carry on with some other task. DOS achieves this by dividing its attention between what you are doing, i.e. the foreground program, and the printing which is the background program. For example, keying at the DOS prompt:

PRINT C:\ACCTS\ACCTTRAN C:\LETTERS\AUNTIEM.DOC ENTER

will print the two files specified (note that they do not have to be in the same directory) while allowing the user to do something else.

5) Buy a faster printer: if none of the methods outlined above reduces your printing bottleneck to a manageable state, you may simply have to purchase a faster printer. If you are already using a high-speed matrix printer, it could be time to consider a laser.

FURTHER PRINTING TIPS

Don't tear off continuous stationery too near the platen; wait till a few more sheets have printed, or until the whole job is complete. Yanking the paper can spoil the printout or even damage the printhead or feeding mechanism

Don't leave continuous labels unused in your printer for any length of time; if left they will stick to the platen

Don't pile manuals and papers on top of your printer; they could break the plastic cover or, if the power is on, cause overheating

Make a careful record of all printer settings and configuration details, including driver details

Keep the printer clean. Dust covers are available for printers as well as computers (do make sure the printer is switched off, or else it will overheat). Matrix printer printheads and daisywheels should be cleaned occasionally with special kits designed for the purpose. Paper particles, carbon from ribbons and dust all accumulate inside a printer; switch it off and hoover inside every few months

Always keep adequate consumable stocks. Use good quality paper and ribbons. Remember to order any printed stationery well before running out. If you use a daisywheel printer, always keep a spare printwheel: they do break eventually

TROUBLESHOOTING

If you are getting no output at all, check: is the printer plugged in, connected to the PC, switched on, and on-line? Has output been redirected for any reason e.g. to the serial port? If so, you may need to use the DOS MODE command to switch it back again. For a parallel printer, type in:

MODE LPT1:,,P ENTER

If you are getting faint, smudged or distorted print, check: is the ribbon on its last legs? Has the printhead been cleaned recently? If the printer is heavily used, the printhead could simply be wearing out: it is typically the first component to fail but can be replaced.

If nothing changes when you alter printer settings, you may need to switch the printer's power off and back on again before the new settings are recognised. If you sent control codes, are you sure they were correct?

If your printer 'hiccups' or misses an occasional character, it could be a loose connection, or because your PC is sending output faster than your printer can cope with it; sometimes you may get an error message like 'Error writing to device' or 'Device timeout'. Try keying in the MODE command, exactly as above, at the DOS prompt. It ensures that your PC keeps on trying to send data to the printer until the printer has caught up.

If your printer needs professional servicing, re-pack it for transportation in the original materials; keep them just in case. The printhead of some printers needs securing before the machine is moved.

A final printing tip: do not throw away your typewriter. An individual or small organisation can be paralysed if its sole means of producing letters or other documents is a PC printer. Somebody must still remember how to use a typewriter - and correction fluid!

 Keep your typewriter!

Chapter Eight
Time-Saving Techniques

BATCH FILES

Most PC users find that they frequently use a set sequence of MS-DOS commands: each time they load and run a particular applications program, for example. When each command has to be individually typed, the whole sequence can take some time. Any errors in entering commands, even if they do not actually cause damage, may necessitate going back to the beginning of the sequence again. This tedious business can be automated by using batch files, consisting of a series of predetermined MS-DOS commands, all of which are carried out in sequence by simply typing in the name of the file. All batch files must be of filetype .BAT so that MS-DOS knows that it contains commands to be executed.

Suppose that a PC user frequently switches from, say, accounts to word processing. The word processing package (let's call it Supaword) allows the mouse to be used, and this user has a serial printer attached. The following commands therefore have to be typed in, each time this particular user starts word processing:

```
CHDIR C:\SYS ENTER
MOUSE ENTER
MODE LPT1:=COM1: ENTER
CHDIR C:\WORDPROC ENTER
SUPAWORD ENTER
```

If, instead of typing them in separately, these exact command lines are placed in a file called, say, WP.BAT - all the user needs to type is: WP ENTER to achieve the same results. Many commands can be automatically carried out in this way; batch files can also enable you to display information, remind the user what to do next, test conditions before carrying out certain commands and to choose between different options - without typing in a single command!

Store often-used command sequences in a batch file, rather than keying them in separately each time

HOW TO CREATE A BATCH FILE

The quickest way to set up a batch file is to enter it directly from the computer screen. For the above example, you would first type in:

COPY CON C:WP.BAT ENTER

which tells the PC to copy whatever is keyed in straight to a file called WP.BAT (on drive C). Everything you type subsequently will be written to the WP batch file. The commands you want in the file are then carefully entered as above, pressing return after each one; to end input press the F6 key (which is equivalent to holding down the Ctrl key and pressing Z). Ctrl-Z, which will appear as ^Z on your PC screen, is an end of file marker; finally, pressing return will copy all the commands to the batch file and return you to the DOS prompt. COPY CON is a quick way to create files, but once you have keyed in a line and hit ENTER, you can no longer change or edit that line, so your typing has to be totally accurate.

Using an editor program to create batch files

To set up batch files containing more than three or four commands an editor program should be used, enabling you not only to create files but also to add to or modify them. The program RPED.EXE, supplied with your Amstrad PC (on floppy disk number 3), is an easy-to-use editor program which can cope with files up to 750 lines long - more than enough for the batch files you are likely to require. The program is started by simply keying in: RPED ENTER or, from the GEM Desktop, by double-clicking on the RPED.EXE icon. RPED is quite friendly, showing you which keys to press to create new files or edit existing ones, or how to insert or delete lines within the file currently being edited.

If you ever do need to create files containing thousands of lines, you should probably be using a word processing program, a data base manager or some other applications program. Masochists can use the fairly user-hostile MS-DOS EDLIN editor (on floppy disk 1).

AUTOMATIC STARTING: THE AUTOEXEC.BAT FILE

Batch files like the WP.BAT file example above can save you a minute or two every single time you start a particular program: that soon mounts up. A little more time is saved by automating the startup process still more with the AUTOEXEC.BAT file, which can give you a flying start into any application - without keying in any commands.

When you first start up your PC the operating system automatically carries out several checks, including looking to see if there is a file called AUTOEXEC.BAT on disk (on whichever drive your system normally reads while starting up). If there is such a file, the commands within it are automatically obeyed, without your having to lift a finger! The same applies when you re-start ('warmstart') your PC (with the Ctrl, Alt and Del keys). The process of installing commercial software (including GEM products) on your PC often sets up an AUTOEXEC.BAT file for you. Check your disk directories to see if you have one; you can quickly examine its contents with the TYPE command. It may contain any valid MS-DOS command, including for instance:

REM (to include remarks in the file which explain its purpose and operation)

PROMPT (to give more information at the DOS prompt, telling the user which is the default directory, for example)

CHDIR (to change the default directory)

PATH (to tell DOS where i.e. which disks/directories to look at, in order to find your program files)

KEYBUK (to ensure that the keyboard is set to UK characters)

MOUSE (not strictly an MS-DOS command, this sets up the mouse for use with the application)

MODE (to set up the printer or communications links)

CLS (to clear the screen)

ECHO (to display messages to the user, or request input)

IF (to enable an action to be carried out only if some condition is met)

GOTO (to enable lines in the batch file to be skipped if required)

FOR (enables repetition of actions in batch files)

PAUSE (to wait for the user to carry out some requested action e.g. switch disks, confirm that the next action is required)

DATE (to enable the user to reset the date: not usually needed for your Amstrad as your battery-backed RAM should remember the date. You will, however, usually include the RTC command which runs a little program to tell DOS the time and date according to your Amstrad's battery-backed RAM)

filename (where the file is of type EXE or COM - or another BAT file; this will execute the relevant program or batch file, to load an application or carry out other required instructions)

All these (and other DOS commands) can be executed from within an AUTOEXEC.BAT file. Examples of the practical use of all of these commands will be seen below; your Amstrad (or MS-DOS) manual gives complete details of how to enter each command. Normally a program name, or that of another batch file, is included as a final command (if it is a BAT file it must come last) to start your chosen application automatically. The filetype (EXE, COM or BAT) should be omitted. For example:

```
REM ****************** AUTOEXEC.BAT *********************
PATH C:\;A:\;B:\
PROMPT $p$g
KEYBUK
MOUSE
MODE LPT1:,,P
ANYPROG
REM ******************* END OF FILE **********************
```

carries out the following tasks:

1) The PATH command tells the system to look on drive C, drive A and drive B for program files. These include external MS-DOS commands i.e. those which are stored on disk. It is often useful to be able to find these without changing the directory.
2) The PROMPT command will display the current directory on the default drive, followed by a > character e.g. C:\ACCOUNTS>
3) KEYBUK ensures that the keyboard is set to the UK standard: e.g. £ sign is SHIFT 3, etc.
4) MOUSE sets your Amstrad mouse to work with the program (as long as the program was designed for mouse control)
5) The MODE command in this case ensures that the system will keep on trying to send data to the (parallel) printer, even if the printer is too busy to receive it. This is useful if your printer is rather slow and has no built-in print buffer.
6) Finally, ANYPROG runs the ANYPROG application program (a real program name would be inserted here).

Existing AUTOEXEC.BAT files can be altered with RPED or EDLIN; otherwise you can write your own files from scratch (the above example should give you something to work on). If you are running programs from floppy disk you can write a specific AUTO-EXEC file for each program disk: e.g. one to start up word processing, one to start up your data base, etc.

This should minimise tiresome floppy swapping, especially if a system disk is used i.e. one FORMATted with the /S option to include system files on the disk. If the relevant application program and any necessary associated files, as well as the AUTOEXEC.BAT file, are stored together on such a disk, starting up and running the application automatically from a single disk should be possible. See chapter 10 for more details on making 'startup' disks. Hard disk users may have several programs, each in its own directory on the hard disk. They can have many BAT files, but only one AUTOEXEC.BAT file will be recognised on the hard disk; it must be on the root directory. It can, however, enable you to choose from a menu of program options, as we shall see below.

 Carefully set up, AUTOEXEC files can save as much as 10 minutes every day; for most PC users, this is equivalent to gaining an extra four or five complete working days every year!

OTHER TIME-SAVING BATCH FILES

Finding mislaid information

Batch files can streamline many other tasks. We saw in chapter 6 how to use the FIND command to look for mislaid text in one or two files - but if you are, say, searching an entire directory and have no idea where your missing information might be, this can be very tedious. The following batch file will search *every* file in the directory for a particular string of characters.

Note the extensive use of REM statements to explain how the batch file command works; there is actually only a single DOS command line doing all the work. You can set up this file exactly as shown (using RPED or EDLIN), calling it FINDTEXT.BAT and making sure that the FIND.EXE command is also available on disk.

```
REM ******************** FINDTEXT.BAT **********************
REM *** searches an entire directory with the FIND command
REM ********************************************************
REM ** Command format is FINDTEXT string filespec /switch
REM **
REM ** where string represents the characters being sought,
REM ** filespec is the file or range of files to examine,
REM ** and /switch is one or more of:
REM ** /C (to print the count of lines in each file
REM ** which matched the required string) or
REM ** /N (to print the line number of matching lines,
REM ** counting from the start of each file) or
REM ** /V (to display all lines NOT containing the
REM ** required string of characters).
REM ** The IF clause prevents doing a FIND on FIND.EXE
REM ********************************************************
REM *
FOR %%A IN (%2) DO  IF NOT FIND.EXE = =%%A   FIND %3 %1 %%A
REM *
REM ******************** END OF FILE **********************
```

To use this batch file, type the following at the DOS prompt:

```
FINDTEXT "groundnut oil" *.* /N ENTER
```

and the system will search every file (represented by *.*) in the current directory to see if it can find the phrase "groundnut oil". The % symbols serve to pass the details you key in as 'parameters' after the FINDTEXT command - into the batch file itself. Thus "groundnut oil", the first parameter, becomes %1 and so on. This process will display each filename as it searches and if a match is found will show you the line number where it occurs in that file and display the line itself. The output will look something like:

```
------------ FIN9999.DOC
[127] clear that investment opportunities for groundnut oil are now
[143] health food industry, groundnut oil has a strong position as
```

Remember that FIND will match the string exactly. Therefore to pick up every reference, perhaps including instances where the phrase begins a sentence ("Groundnut oil is ideal for stir-frying ....") you could search for a shorter string, without the initial capital letter, e.g. "roundnut oil". You can limit the search to, say, files of type .DOC by specifying *.DOC instead of *.*; if you only need to search one or two files you might as well use the FIND command directly, as described in chapter 6.

If you ever mislay a portion of text, a batch file like FINDTEXT will rapidly search an entire directory to locate it

By the way, the FIND command objects violently to examining itself. Therefore the FINDTEXT file above automatically checks each filename before executing a FIND to ensure that it never tries to operate on the FIND.EXE file itself.

AUTOMATED PC USAGE RECORDS

You may find it helpful, especially if several different people have access to your PC, to keep a user log with details such as the date and time each time the PC is started up, along with the user's name and the purpose of each session. Many people maintain such logs manually; here is a way, particularly useful for hard disk users, to automate the process. This example assumes that the user log will be stored on the root directory of drive C. The following commands can be placed in a special LOGON.BAT file, but it is perhaps better to put them into your AUTOEXEC.BAT file, so that logging on is automatically carried out every time the PC is switched on or reset.

```
ECHO OFF
REM **************** LOGGING ON PROCEDURE ****************
REM *** automatically writes the date and time to a user log
REM *** and asks users for their name and purpose of session
REM ********************************************************
REM *
CLS
DATE > > USER.LOG < ENTCHAR
TIME > > USER.LOG < ENTCHAR
ECHO *** Please type your first and last names (and Enter)
ECHO *** Then type the purpose of this PC session (and Enter)
ECHO *** Finally, press the F6 key (and Enter)
COPY CON TEMP.USR
TYPE TEMP.USR > > USER.LOG
DEL TEMP.USR
REM ********************** END OF FILE **********************
```

Before these batch file commands will work a file called ENTCHAR, containing just one 'Enter' or carriage return, must be set up; this is used to feed, via '< ENTCHAR', an automatic carriage return to the DATE and TIME commands in the batch file.

Create the ENTCHAR file as follows:

```
COPY CON C:ENTCHAR ENTER
ENTER
[F6] ENTER    (i.e. press the F6 function key, then the ENTER key)
```

Every week or two you might like to print out the USER.LOG to obtain a permanent record. You can then free some space by deleting it; the batch commands given will re-create the USER.LOG file if it does not exist.

 An automated user log can contribute to:
a) reliable monitoring of computer usage
b) analysis of future hardware and software needs
c) troubleshooting

AUTOMATING BACKUPS

Making backups is of course vital, but it can seem such a chore that sooner or later you or your colleagues may succumb to temptation, perhaps delaying the job or missing out the odd one altogether. That of course is the exact moment when disaster will strike. Setting up a backup batch file can take some of the donkeywork out of backups. Better still, you can set up a batch file to backup your files automatically after every program run.

Suppose you normally run your usual application: accounts, word processing, etc. by simply keying in the program name: let's call it ANYPROG. Twin floppy disk users would typically keep the program disk in drive A and the data disk in drive B. There are many ways to set up a backup file; a good way to reduce disk swapping is to place two batch files on the program disk in drive A as follows:

```
ECHO OFF
REM *********************** START.BAT *************************
REM ***   This file is used to start up the ANYPROG program
REM ***********************************************************
REM *
ECHO ON
ANYPROG
COPY A:BKUP.BAT B:
COPY ENTCHAR B:
B:
BKUP
REM ********************** END OF FILE ************************
```

```
ECHO OFF
REM ************************* BKUP.BAT *************************
CLS
ECHO ******************* Backup Procedure ********************
ECHO .
REM extra lines for backup logging can go here (see below)
ECHO .
ECHO Please remove your program disk from drive A
ECHO .
ECHO ... and place your backup disk in drive A
ECHO .
ECHO You can stop this backup process by holding down Ctrl and
ECHO simultaneously pressing C. Otherwise...
ECHO .
ECHO ... Please check carefully that the correct backup disk
ECHO . is in drive A - all files on A are about to be deleted
ECHO .
PAUSE
REM ****** Clear space on A for storage of backup files *********
ECHO ON
FOR %%A IN (A:*.*) DO DEL %%A
COPY B:*.* A:
ECHO OFF
ECHO .
ECHO Backup process completed.  Please record details in
ECHO the backup log, and store the backup disk carefully.
ECHO .
REM ********************* END OF FILE *************************
```

These two files work as follows. To start running ANYPROG, the user simply types in: START ENTER. The START batch file runs the ANYPROG program and remains in control when the user has finished with ANYPROG. The BKUP.BAT file is then copied on to drive B: this is to allow for the fact that any number of separate data disks might be in use. It cannot be left on drive A because the program disk will shortly have to be removed to make room for the backup disk. The START file makes sure that B is the default drive and starts the backup procedure itself by running the BKUP.BAT file.

BKUP.BAT begins by asking the user to remove the program disk (ANYPROG) from drive A, then to insert a backup disk into drive A. When the user is sure that the correct disk is in A, all files on it are deleted to leave an empty disk to receive backup files. Finally, all the files on B are copied to A; details are displayed as the files are copied.

The user is reminded to update the 'backup log', stating which disk has been used and when - remember the recommendation to use a number of backup disks in strict rotation? Many users find a manual log quite adequate, but if you really hate clerical chores even this can be automated.

Automatic Backup Log

Suppose you have four backup floppies, used in rotation to give you, for example, copies of your accounts files as they stood at the end on Friday afternoon of the last four weeks. Batch commands can be used to keep a simple log and to tell you which disk to use next. Make sure that you have enough room on your default drive/ directory to keep your backup log file and that the little ENTCHAR file we used earlier (containing just a carriage return character) is still available. Then the following commands can be inserted into your backup batch file (e.g. at the point indicated by the REM statement near the beginning of BKUP.BAT, see above):

```
REM *** Commands to update backup log and advise user as to
REM *** which backup disk is the next one to use in the cycle
REM ***
IF EXIST LASTBKUP.4 GOTO BACKUP1
IF EXIST LASTBKUP.1 GOTO BACKUP2
IF EXIST LASTBKUP.2 GOTO BACKUP3
IF EXIST LASTBKUP.3 GOTO BACKUP4
ECHO NEW BACKUP LOG FILE CREATED ON: > > LASTBKUP.4
DATE > > LASTBKUP.4 < ENTCHAR
TIME > > LASTBKUP.4 < ENTCHAR
:BACKUP1
REN LASTBKUP.4 LASTBKUP.1
ECHO BACKUP FROM ANYPROG TO DISK 1 - CARRIED OUT ON: > >
LASTBKUP.1
ECHO . Backup Disk 1 should be used for this backup procedure
DATE > > LASTBKUP.1 < ENTCHAR
TIME > > LASTBKUP.1 < ENTCHAR
GOTO BACKEND
:BACKUP2
REN LASTBKUP.1 LASTBKUP.2
ECHO BACKUP FROM ANYPROG TO DISK 2 - CARRIED OUT ON: > >
LASTBKUP.2
ECHO . Backup Disk 2 should be used for this backup procedure
DATE > > LASTBKUP.2 < ENTCHAR
TIME > > LASTBKUP.2 < ENTCHAR
GOTO BACKEND
```

(commands continue overleaf...)

```
:BACKUP3
REN LASTBKUP.2 LASTBKUP.3
ECHO BACKUP FROM ANYPROG TO DISK 3 - CARRIED OUT ON: > >
LASTBKUP.3
ECHO . Backup Disk 3 should be used for this backup procedure
DATE > > LASTBKUP.3 < ENTCHAR
TIME > > LASTBKUP.3 < ENTCHAR
GOTO BACKEND
:BACKUP4
REN LASTBKUP.3 LASTBKUP.4
ECHO BACKUP FROM ANYPROG TO DISK 4 - CARRIED OUT ON: > >
LASTBKUP.4
ECHO . Backup Disk 4 should be used for this backup procedure
DATE > > LASTBKUP.4 < ENTCHAR
TIME > > LASTBKUP.4 < ENTCHAR
:BACKEND
```

There is no easy way to increase a counter, and act according to its value, in an MS-DOS batch file. These commands achieve the desired result by using the actual filename of the backup log to indicate which disk was last used in the backup cycle. Here's how it works. The default directory is checked to see if the backup log is on disk and, if so, what its name is: if, for example, LASTBKUP.2 exists then the PC will advise the user that backup disk number 3 should be used for the current backup procedure. Then some lines are written to the backup log, showing that disk 3 was used, together with the date and time of the backup procedure. Finally the whole backup log file is renamed LASTBKUP.3, so that next time round the system will tell the user to use backup disk 4, and so on.

Remember that the above commands should be embedded into a batch file such as BKUP.BAT above, so that the backup itself proceeds automatically. Every so often, as with the user log file, you might want to print out the backup log for reference, for added security and/or to free some space by deleting the log file (LASTBKUP.?) itself. The above commands will automatically create a new log file if none exists. The routine can easily be amended to allow for fewer or more disks in the backup cycle.

Automated backups for single floppy disk users

A batch file such as BKUP.BAT will work perfectly well for users with single disk (SD) Amstrad models. They may have to replace their program disk in the drive in order to start up the backup procedure, unless their applications programs are loaded into a RAM disk for normal operation. Thereafter the PC will announce when disks should be changed; the disk drive serves as drive A and drive B in turn. More ECHO statements can be added to clarify the procedure or to give further instructions to the operator.

Automated backups for hard disk users

Experience suggests that the BACKUP and RESTORE commands (designed primarily for hard disk users) can be confusing and troublesome to many people. A full disk backup takes a lot of disks and quite a lot of time; the 'switches' which can be used with these commands require considerable care. There are, however, useful options, including backing up only those files which have changed since a specified date, a backup log file, etc. See your Amstrad manual for details. On balance, less experienced users are advised to avoid BACKUP and RESTORE. Using simple COPY commands is, in any event, often faster - especially if, as suggested, they are built into your normal operating procedures, preferably by automatic batch file commands. A file like the BKUP.BAT file above can be used; it would of course have to refer to drive C, etc.

Most users find that, for a given application (typically using one directory), all their data files will in fact fit on to a single floppy disk for backup purposes. Otherwise, all files of a particular filetype can be saved together. For example, an integrated package of accounting programs might use filetype .MAS for all the master files and filetype .TRN for all the transaction files; the user could include the following commands in a backup batch file:

```
CLS
ECHO **************** Accounts Backup Procedure ******************
ECHO .
ECHO . Please place your backup disk for accounts MASTER files
ECHO . in drive A
PAUSE
ECHO .
ECHO . Please check carefully that the correct backup disk
ECHO . is in drive A - all files on A are about to be deleted
ECHO .
PAUSE
ECHO ON
FOR %%A IN (A:*.*) DO DEL %%A
```

(commands continue overleaf)

```
COPY C:*.MAS A:
ECHO .
ECHO . Master File Backup process completed.
ECHO .
ECHO . Please place your backup disk for accounts TRANSACTION files
ECHO . in drive A
ECHO .
PAUSE
ECHO .
ECHO . Please check carefully that the correct backup disk
ECHO . is in drive A - all files on A are about to be deleted
ECHO .
PAUSE
FOR %%A  IN (A:*.*) DO DEL %%A
COPY C:*.TRN A:
ECHO .
ECHO . Transaction File Backup process completed.
ECHO .
ECHO . Please record details in the Backup Log and store
ECHO . the Backup disks carefully
```

 Automating your backups is another significant time-saver. Even more importantly, it will ensure that timely backups are never skipped

You may still find, despite using batch files to facilitate regular backups, that they are getting too time-consuming, especially if you need to use a number of floppy disks to complete the process. A number of 'go-faster' backup utility programs, with names like Fastback and Jetback, are available for hard disk users who find that they need to take frequent backups. The ultimate solution, if the volumes and rate of change of your data justify it, may be to invest in additional hardware (e.g. a tape streamer) to make regular backups easier and safer.

SCREEN MENUS

When you want to set up a variety of options for yourself (or colleagues) to choose from, it is far better to provide a menu of possible choices on screen than to have to remember particular commands or sequences. If you are using GEM-based software, or your programs can at least be configured under GEM, you can choose by double-clicking on the appropriate icon. But for many of the most popular PC programs, you may load and run directly from

DOS: either you must remember the exact command sequences, or you must devise some kind of menu. Readers with programming expertise may be able to use their favourite language to devise menus; several 'menu-generator' programs are available, some at low cost from user groups.

MS-DOS batch files can also be employed for this task. As an example, suppose a hard disk PC user wants a quick way of selecting between word processing, accounts, spreadsheet or communications programs; let's call them SUPAWORD, MAXILEDGER, 3-2-1 and POLYLINK. Each program with its associated files is kept in a separate directory; these are called WORDPROC, AC-COUNTS, SPREAD and COMMS. One of the simplest ways of setting up a menu for these options is to use the following batch commands, preferably as part of the AUTOEXEC.BAT file discussed earlier:

```
ECHO OFF
REM **************** USER MENU COMMANDS ******************
REM ********************************************************
REM *** These commands enable the user to choose an application
REM *** from a screen menu by keying in a single letter (A - D)
REM ********************************************************
CLS
ECHO **************** APPLICATIONS MENU ********************
ECHO .
ECHO Please choose your application by pressing (A-D) then ENTER
ECHO .
ECHO .        A - SupaWord Word Processing
ECHO .
ECHO .        B - MaxiLedger Integrated Accounts
ECHO .
ECHO .        C - 3-2-1 Spreadsheet
ECHO .
ECHO .        D - Polylink Communications
ECHO .
```

To complete this little menu system, you would create four little batch files on the root directory, called A.BAT, B.BAT, C.BAT and D.BAT. They might look something like those overleaf, depending of course on the individual commands required to load and run each program. In operation, starting up the PC would cause the AUTOEXEC.BAT file to display the menu, the user would simply press, say, B - then ENTER and immediately the accounts software would be up and running.

Examples of batch files to complete the menu system:

```
ECHO OFF
REM *************************** A.BAT ***************************
REM *** Batch file to load SupaWord Word Processing Software
REM ************************************************************
CHDIR C:\SYS
MOUSE
MODE LPT1:=COM1:
CHDIR C:\WORDPROC
SW
REM ********************* END OF FILE **********************

ECHO OFF
REM *************************** B.BAT ***************************
REM ***   Batch file to load Maxiledger Integrated Accounts
REM ************************************************************
CHDIR C.\ACCOUNTS
MAXIL
REM ********************* END OF FILE **********************
```

 If you regularly use two or more different applications, adding a menu facility to the startup procedure can save another minute, every time you run a program

PRINTER CONTROL

As we mentioned briefly in the last chapter, batch files can be used to send special control codes to your printer, which your word processing or other applications program may not be able to provide directly. These codes may be required to compress or expand print, to start or stop italics, enlarged print, change typefaces, character pitch, proportional spacing, bidirectional print, etc. The actual codes needed do vary from printer to printer; one example we used was turning on condensed print for a typical Epson printer with a batch file containing the ASCII character 015. We now know how simple it is to create such a file:

```
COPY CON COND.BAT ENTER
ECHO OFF ENTER
ECHO [Alt] 015 > PRN ENTER
ECHO = = = Condensed Print Now On = = = ENTER
[F6] ENTER
```

The ASCII 015 is entered by holding down the Alt key, tapping out 015 on the numeric keypad, then releasing Alt. Similar batch files can be set up for any other printer function. One minor problem is that printer codes often include ESC characters (ASCII code 27) - indeed they are often called Escape Codes. Now MS-DOS sulks if you try to key in ESC characters; it just will not accept them. One solution is to use the alternative code for ESC, which is ASCII code 155 (27 + 128: the high-order bit is 1, for anyone interested in binary matters). MS-DOS will swallow this quite happily, while your printer (*most* models ignore high-order bits) still recognises it as an ESC character. So, for example, to set Epson-compatible line spacing to 8 lines per inch:

```
COPY CON 8LPI.BAT ENTER
ECHO OFF ENTER
ECHO [Alt]155O > PRN ENTER
ECHO = = = Line Spacing Now Set to 8 Lines per Inch = = = ENTER
[F6] ENTER
```

This file sends an ESC-O control sequence to the printer. Another file, probably called 6LPI.BAT, would contain an ESC-2 sequence, which switches the printer back to 6 lines per inch. Once you have set up as many batch files as you need (your printer manual should tell you all the available codes) it is a simple matter to choose them from a menu as shown earlier. You can invite the operator to key in the names we have used e.g. COND, 6LPI etc. or instead call the batch files A.BAT, B.BAT,... or even 1.BAT, 2.BAT,... as long as you have not already used those names before.

More About RAM Disks

A RAM disk can be a major time-saver, especially for floppy disk users. The reason is simple: after printing, disk accessing is by far the slowest activity on your PC. Those few seconds of delay, every single time you read or write to a floppy disk, and that includes loading chunks of program, help files, etc. as well as your data, soon mount up to minutes and hours wasted. The simulated 'disk' in RAM, by contrast, works almost instantaneously.

 A RAM disk can dramatically speed up most PC operations

The major drawback, as we saw in chapter 5, is that RAM is volatile: all your RAM disk files are lost when you switch off your PC, unless you have remembered to copy them to a real disk before switching off. Some programs (e.g. WordStar 1512/1640) at least remind you about your RAM disk files as you are exiting from the program; the following method will enable you to set any program up so that you cannot forget to make those copies. Once again you can modify your AUTOEXEC.BAT file, to make it copy COMMAND.COM to the RAM disk, along with a new batch file called, say, WPSTART.BAT. This second file includes commands for automatic copying of any files on RAM disk across to a floppy disk. If you are using, say, SupaWord on a twin floppy disk PC, your AUTOEXEC file would perhaps include the following commands:

```
REM *** Copy COMMAND.COM to RAM disk
COPY A:COMMAND.COM C:
SET COMSPEC=C:\COMMAND.COM
REM *** Change default drive
C:
REM *** Copy batch file to RAM disk
COPY A:WPSTART.BAT C:
REM *** Run batch file
WPSTART
```

The WPSTART.BAT file itelf would contain commands to copy the program and associated files on to the RAM disk so as to speed up operation, then actually run it. When you exit the program, any files which you have created (on the RAM disk) are automatically copied on to floppy disk. These commands will do the job:

```
ECHO OFF
REM ********************* WPSTART.BAT ***********************
CLS
REM ****** Copy SupaWord Program, Overlay and Help files
ECHO Copying Program files to RAM disk ...
ECHO .
REM ****** (to modify this procedure for your own use,
REM ****** check your software manual to see the names of
REM ****** the files which you need available for your
REM ****** particular program, then change the names in
REM ****** the following COPY commands accordingly)
COPY A:SW.EXE C:
COPY A:SW.OV1 C:
COPY A:SWHELP.DAT C:
REM ****** Place data disk in drive B
ECHO Please put a data disk in drive B to store your files
```

```
ECHO Make sure that there is enough space on the disk in B
ECHO for any files you create
ECHO .
PAUSE
ECHO If you want to load an existing file into RAM for
ECHO addition or amendment, use the SupaWord copy option
ECHO to copy the file to drive C before you start editing it
PAUSE
REM ****** Run SupaWord Program ******************************
SW
REM ****** Automatically copy data files from RAM disk
CLS
ECHO Copying files from RAM disk to drive B ...
ECHO .
REM ****** First remove RAM disk copies of SupaWord files
REM ****** (change names depending on your program)
DEL C:SW.EXE
DEL C:SW.OV1
DEL C:SWHELP.DAT
ECHO ON
REM ****** Copy any new files from RAM disk to floppy in B
FOR %%A IN (C:*.*) IF NOT COMMAND.COM = = %%A DO COPY %%A B:
ECHO OFF
REM ********************** END OF FILE ************************
```

The program filenames used above are of course for illustration only; they must be replaced by the files required by your particular application. The suggested commands can easily be modified for users of PCs with only a single floppy disk, who will need to remove their program disks once the program(s) are loaded into the RAM disk, in order to load a data disk.

Hard disk users tend not to bother with RAM disks, because disk access speeds are so much better than with floppies. However, accessing RAM disk is as much as ten times faster than accessing even a hard disk, so should not be ruled out. The author normally works on hard disk machines but still makes extensive use of RAM disks. Amstrad recommend cutting out any RAM disk when running GEM-based applications on a hard disk. A special utility program NVRPAT2 is supplied to cut your RAM disk to zero. For many applications, however, including most DOS-based programs:

 Hard disk users, too, can make time savings with a RAM disk.

Remember that the above example, with WPSTART.BAT, ensures only that you have one permanent copy of files you create on RAM disk. Even with this safeguard, you should still copy your data files on to floppy every so often during a PC session. Moreover, for real security, you still need to make backups on to a separate disk. It is recommended that, as before, the backup procedure is also automated.

How Large a RAM Disk?

The procedures suggested above, for copying your program and the files it uses on to RAM disk for extra-fast operation, will obviously work only if the RAM disk is large enough. Some programs are just too big; to check this, simply add up the sizes (as shown in the directory) of all the files required. Even if the program(s) will not fit, a RAM disk used only to store your data files can still speed operations considerably.

If you are using the GEM Desktop, along with the GEM accessories, on a 512K PC, you will not be able to use a RAM disk larger than 34K. While this may be large enough for some data files, there are not many programs which will squeeze into this alongside their data files. This leaves you three options:

a) Stick to GEM applications only (with minimum or 0 RAM disk)
b) Upgrade your RAM to 640K (PC 1640 users already have 640K)
c) Leave the GEM environment to make full use of RAM and/or RAM disk with DOS-based applications

Option (a) has now become feasible, as more GEM-based software has been released. However, some of the most powerful packages are not available to GEM users, and the sheer volume of MS-DOS software is vast. Option (b) may allow you to get the best of both worlds, keeping all the ease of use of GEM with the option to switch to MS-DOS and enjoy a fairly healthy 160K or so of RAM disk: enough to enable lightning-fast use of many packages. 1512 users may need to load GEM from MS-DOS, by typing GEM at the MS-DOS prompt, in order to gain this flexibility. Many users will opt for (c). Far more packages are available for MS-DOS than for any other operating system. Sometimes their performance is greatly improved by running them from RAM disk; other packages need to use directly a large proportion of your RAM in order to run at all.

Setting the RAM disk size

Your Amstrad can remember a suitable size for the RAM disk, by storing the size in the battery-backed non-volatile RAM (NVR): the same gadget that remembers the time and date for you. This size value can easily be changed by running the NVR utility; the NVR.EXE file is situated in the root directory on your GEM desktop disk. To run this program, simply key in: NVR ENTER. Use the cursor keys or the space bar to select the 'Size of RAM disk' option, then press ENTER. When you have entered the required RAM disk size (an even whole number) you will be given the option to save this (and any other) change to the NVR. The next time you start up (or warmstart) your system, it will take the new value for the RAM disk size.

It is not very convenient to have to run this utility program every time you want to change the size of RAM disk - especially if you are using several different applications programs, each requiring different RAM disk sizes. There is a faster way to tackle this task; to take advantage of this we must understand the function of the vital CONFIG.SYS file.

We saw earlier how, when you start your PC under MS-DOS, it always looks to see if there is an AUTOEXEC.BAT file in the root directory: if so, the commands within that file are automatically obeyed. Well, at the same time, MS-DOS also looks for the CONFIG.SYS file, which contains crucial information. If you examine it (e.g. by TYPEing the file) you will see something like:

```
COUNTRY=044
FILES=20
BUFFERS=5
DEVICE=RAMDRIVE.SYS NVR
```

Let us look at that last command first; it installs the 'ramdrive device driver'. In plainer English, it tells the system that you want to use a RAM disk; furthermore, it tells the system to go and look at the NVR, which will tell it how much RAM to set aside as RAM disk. Instead, you can write a specific value in the command, e.g.:

```
DEVICE=RAMDRIVE.SYS 100
```

will set up a 100K RAM disk, no matter what the NVR says.

Now suppose you have, as suggested earlier, a separate 'startup' disk for each of your applications. Each will probably contain an AUTOEXEC.BAT file, so why not have a separate CONFIG.SYS file on each disk too; then each application can start with the ideal size of RAM disk (if any). Users (including those with hard disks) who wish to maintain the flexibility to change the RAM disk to any size can use a batch file such as the following:

```
ECHO OFF
REM ************* RAMSET.BAT ***************
REM *** batch file to set RAM disk easily
DEL CONFIG.SYS
ECHO FILES=20>>CONFIG.SYS
ECHO BUFFERS=10>>CONFIG.SYS
ECHO COUNTRY=044>>CONFIG.SYS
ECHO DEVICE=RAMDRIVE.SYS %1>>CONFIG.SYS
ECHO Now restart the PC (Ctrl Alt Del)
REM ************* END OF FILE *************
```

This file simply deletes and re-creates the CONFIG.SYS file so that subsequent restarting of the PC will set up a RAM disk of the required size. To create a 160K RAM disk, for example, key in: RAMSET 160 ENTER and then reset the PC. This is much quicker than running the NVR program. The other commands commonly used in the CONFIG.SYS file are also important. The FILES command tells your system the maximum number of files which your program(s) might need to handle at any given time: this is more than you might think. Many word processing programs, some spreadsheets, accounts, graphics and other packages need to set up temporary disk files during their operation. Add these to the program and associated files (the package may use several at once) and your files are soon into double figures. Therefore it is a sensible to include in your CONFIG.SYS file, say: FILES=20.

The BUFFERS command also helps with file handling. A buffer is an intermediate area of storage, used to ease the flow of data between two devices. Just as a printer buffer can release your PC's processor from slow printers sooner, so the BUFFERS command speeds up *disk* input and output, usually a major PC bottleneck. With no BUFFERS command, the system automatically sets up two buffers in RAM, together taking up about 1K. Programs which frequently read and write disks, especially floppies, will run considerably faster with, say, BUFFERS=15 in the CONFIG.SYS file. Bear in mind that this will take up about 8K of RAM.

COUNTRY is the other command commonly included in the CONFIG.SYS file. It controls the conventions for the date, number display and currency, depending upon the country which you specify. For example, American dates put the month before the day (MMDDYY) as opposed to the UK (DDMMYY), while the French use a comma where we place a decimal point, and so on. The country codes resemble the international telephone dialling codes. Thus the UK is 044, the USA is 001, Germany 049, Netherlands 031, France 033 and so on. The command to set your PC for the UK is therefore: COUNTRY = 044. Note that this command will *not* set up the keyboard for a particular country. This is achieved with commands such as KEYBUK, KEYBFR, KEYBGR, etc. - one of which should appear in the MS-DOS AUTOEXEC.BAT file (see above).

FURTHER TIPS

Sometimes it is helpful to make doubly sure that copies of disks or files have been made with 100% accuracy. This extra assurance of correct copying can be obtained in several ways. For disks: DISKCOMP A: B: ENTER will check that the two disks are identical. DISKCOMP will give an error if the copied disk was made with the COPY command rather than with DISKCOPY. Only DISKCOPY makes an identical copy of a disk, whereas COPY A:*.* B: will accurately copy all the files on A on to B, but will not necessarily put them in the same place on B. If COPY is used, whether for single files or a whole disk-full, you can add the /V switch (for Verify) to the original COPY command, e.g.: COPY A:*.* B:*.* /V ENTER will make DOS check the recording of every disk sector written as the copy proceeds. This option slows down the copying process considerably, but you may consider it a sensible precaution, especially if the data concerned is vital.

The VERIFY command will check for correct recording every time you write a file to disk (whether or not you are COPYing). This command, like the /V option with COPY, will slow down the disk writing process. Just type, at the DOS prompt: VERIFY ON ENTER and, when you no longer require verification of every write: VERIFY OFF ENTER. Two files can be compared with the MS-DOS utility program COMP (on disk 1). To compare files line-by-line you can type, for example: COMP FRED ADA ENTER.

Compare disks or files, or use a verification option, when it is important to you that data is written or copied with total accuracy

Tomorrow is another day

Some workoholic readers may have found that, while simultaneously burning the midnight oil and running certain DOS applications, the date fails to move on until the PC has been restarted after midnight. Any files you saved during such a late session were, according to the directory, created at 24:15 pm, 25:30 pm, and so on! This should be cured by running the RTC program, version .3 or later, which will ensure that your application can use the time (and date) stored in your NVR. The RTC.COM program file is supplied on MS-DOS disk 1. If you still have an early version, your dealer or Amstrad will replace it. The best way to ensure that this little program is always run is to make it available on your startup disk, and include the command RTC in your AUTOEXEC.BAT file.

Naming blunders

We have seen the value of carefully chosen filenames in helping you to keep track of your data. Names like FILE, DATA, MYFILE, etc. are virtually certain to cause trouble. Some names, however, are absolutely certain to cause trouble! You must not use device names which are reserved words. For instance, CON means the screen (or, more accurately, the combination of the keyboard and the screen) - the name cannot be used for anything else.

 Don't use device names like AUX, COM1, LPT1, PRN, CON as filenames. Your PC will normally reject them but you may get strange and potentially dangerous results

Chapter Nine
How to Buy Software

For 99.99% of users, buying packaged software is far and away the most cost- and time-effective way of satisfying computing needs. For those who are convinced that they are among the 0.01%, who simply must develop (or have developed) their own software, a word or two of advice will be found towards the end of this chapter. Let us first see how to identify and select good packaged software.

HOW TO CHOOSE

The difficulty much of the time is not a shortage of software, but that there are too many packages on the market which appear to do more or less the same job. Many purchasers of microcomputer packages, faced with such bewildering choice, end up plumping for a particular package as a result of vague impressions or sales claims, often just to get the decision behind them.

But packages do all differ and picking the wrong one can be a costly, frustrating business. On the other hand, some people get bogged down in time-consuming, convoluted selection procedures, with complex checklists and lengthy questionnaires, in a fruitless quest for the holy grail of the perfect program. Clearly we should try to be somewhere in the middle, knowing the key questions to ask and trying to insure ourselves against disastrous choices. We'll see some examples later of simple checklists, which may help you to develop your own version.

It is strange how often buyers suspend common sense judgment, when faced with an impressive demonstration or an extravagant claim. The guidelines which follow are not offered as hard-and-fast rules, as they will not all apply in every case; at the very least, they will help you to define and develop your own priorities and criteria.

FIFTEEN GUIDELINES FOR SOFTWARE SELECTION

GUIDELINE 1 : Analyse Your Needs

This may sound blindingly obvious - but it still needs to be done! Before you start examining specific packages in detail, ask yourself questions like:

What are the real objectives for the application you have in mind? How (if at all) are you doing it now? (If you don't know, you may need to spend some time with those who do: colleagues, professional advisers, etc.)
How much time does it take now?
How much time are you (or your colleagues) prepared to spend in the future?
How could you improve this/these procedures - with or without a software package?
How far can you/will you change these procedures, if a new system might require it?
What kind of data must any package handle?
How much data, how will it be obtained, how often, how much will it change over time?
How must it be manipulated/processed?
What results do you want it to produce?
In what form? How often? How accurate?
Which aspects are essential, which merely desirable?
How else could this information be obtained/used?
Who else might already have/might be able to use this information?
Who else will need to be able to use the package?

GUIDELINE 2 : Consider Future Needs As Well

One of the toughest jobs in computing at any level (unless you have a crystal ball) is assessing possible future requirements. A lot of 'people-years' are wasted scrapping existing systems and installing brand new ones. Often the requirements of the new system are not so very far removed from those of the old - but because growth potential and flexibility to cope with unforeseen needs were not built in, the old system has to go.

Let us take some practical examples. A small business, setting up, say, a simple accounting system, should consider whether it would cope with possible expansion as the business grows. This could mean simply expanding in volume terms (higher turnover, more transactions - what are the limits on file sizes?) but is also likely to involve new types of computing. Could an automated payroll or sales ledger be easily integrated with the currently proposed basic accounting system? Or, if international expansion is a possibility, will the system cope with multiple currencies - or would such a step necessitate laborious manual conversions?

The main concern of an individual user embarking on word processing, on the other hand, would probably be how easy the package is to learn and how convenient and reliable in daily use. But consideration might also be given to future options: might the ability to handle scientific symbols or foreign languages become important? Could there be a requirement to feed, say, figures or charts from a spreadsheet or database package into documents for presentation purposes? Could mailing functions e.g. the ability to merge names and addresses with standard letters be of value? Desktop publishing? Electronic mail?

A departmental manager might install a spreadsheet package to assist in preparing budgets and forecasts for his or her particular area. But would that program facilitate, say, comparison or consolidation with another, related, department? Or could it be used in future to access and 'download' figures held on the company's central computer systems?

GUIDELINE 3 : Don't Expect the Earth

Even today there is a tendency to regard a computer system as a panacea to cure all ills. Carefully chosen and implemented, a software package may well save you time or money - and boost the efficiency of you or your organisation. But for every success story like that there is a tale of unfulfilled expectation, disappointment or disaster. Despite the advertising hype attached to some software, no package will eliminate all your systems problems. A sales ledger package may provide tremendous assistance, but data will still have to be gathered, checked and input, debtors will still have to be chased and difficult decisions will still have to be taken.

At the present state of the art, software cannot really think or solve problems for you; it can, however, assist you in doing both. To avoid disappointment:

 Don't expect to find the perfect package

Don't try to computerise everything in a day

In fact, don't try to computerise everything in any event. Choose the best candidate for computerisation and tackle that area first. It is often where the largest volume of data or paperwork is being handled. Almost always, it will be something that takes up a lot of time at the moment. It is clearly absurd to spend money and effort computerising activities which are fairly painless and do not take up much time at the moment.

When you have found what should be the most suitable area, take a long look at it first. You may need to tidy a few things up before you attempt to computerise a system. Remember that the only likely result of computerising chaotic manual systems is chaotic computer systems. Both undermine the efficiency of an organisation; computers just do it more quickly.

GUIDELINE 4 : Don't Pay the Earth

It is perfectly easy for an Amstrad PC user to pay more for a single software package than for the PC itself. Some users will be entirely justified in such purchases: they may need a level of sophistication or specific features which cannot be found in the run-of-the-mill offerings available for a hundred pounds or so.

But the majority of users are emphatically not in this category. Unless your application is exceptionally specialised - or you are exceptionally fastidious - you are in a very healthy buyers' market for applications software. Until low-priced compatibles (most notably the Amstrad PC) came along, software suppliers reaped pretty healthy profits on their offerings, even after allowing for heavy spending on marketing. Anyone who could splash out on an IBM PC (and they tended to be corporate buyers) would not flinch too much at paying several hundred pounds for a good package. The same software vendors have concluded that many Amstrad buyers will not buy software at such price levels. Therefore, if they want a slice of the Amstrad software market, they must launch products for less than £200 - in many cases less than £100. They have generally repackaged their products, stripping out one or two of the fanciest features, and aimed them directly at you. The reason for stripping out those features is to try to protect their 'up-market' sales of the original products. The good news is that, very often, the features they have removed are just not that vital. If they are, the lower-priced, cut-down product simply will not sell aginst its competition. What is more, other software companies are developing products from scratch which are aimed directly at the lower-priced segment of the market; many of these are of excellent quality.

The moral of all this is that you should look at each product on its merits. Don't be offended by the condescending titles: 'Junior' or 'Basic' packages may well have all the features you need. Don't buy the 'Financial Supremo' if the 'Dogsbody Bookkeeper' package does what you want. Equally, don't be put off by the sales pitch with throwaway lines like 'of course, the really serious user will go for ....'

 When buying microcomputer software packages, more expensive does not necessarily mean better

But still be prepared to spend a bit more than you needed to

There are two reasons for this last piece of perverse-sounding advice. Firstly, however clever you become at selecting software, you may sooner or later make a serious mistake. If you have, admit it, cut your losses and buy another program. The cost, in time and frustration alone, of trying to soldier on with a package that is failing to deliver, will be far greater.

Secondly, there may be times when you cannot be sure whether you need features x, y and z. If you go for a package incorporating them, you must pay perhaps £200; if you do without them, perhaps only £150 or even less. Now if you buy the cheaper package - and x, y or z does turn out to be vital, forcing you to replace it, you might have wasted £150. If, on the other hand, you buy the dearer package, even if you never use those extra features, you have bought some insurance against disruption, for the modest premium of £50.

GUIDELINE 5 : Will the Package Do the Job?

When you have given plenty of thought to your current and future computing needs, and perhaps produced a list, you must obviously assess how well various products match up. For example:

a) How closely does the package fit the requirements which you have defined? The glossy brochures about the package will often give you a good idea as to how well the stated features fit. Indeed, the quality and clarity of presentation in this material provides valuable pointers to the probable quality and intelligibility of the software itself. Never rely on the brochures alone, though - at worst they are downright misleading. Reviews in the computer press are often valuable and usually impartial.

b) Will the package handle the volume of data which you will need, now and for the foreseeable future? The manual will usually tell you the maximum file sizes - make sure you allow plenty of room for growth. Some packages can, on paper at least, accept large quantities of data, but really creak under the strain of day-to-day processing with these volumes. Even if the programs still work OK, the time it takes to process the data may simply become unacceptable. For this reason, be very wary of demonstrations of products which show lightning-fast processing speeds - with a mere handful of records.

Many packages e.g. most spreadsheets and several word processing programs keep their data files in RAM while they are in use. This may not be a drawback but in such cases it is vital that the program always displays how much free memory is left. If your typical spreadsheet or word processed document is likely to be larger than can be fitted into RAM - then such RAM-dependent packages are probably non-starters.

c) How flexible is the package? Most systems need to evolve as circumstances change; beware software which seems totally inflexible. To take some examples: There are, at the time of writing, two VAT rates, 0% and 15% which many accounting systems must cater for. But these are by no means immutable: not only can the percentages change but there used to be three different rates in the UK - and there might be again! Could the proposed package take that in its stride, or would you have to hope that the supplier would issue an update in time?

It is not enough to be able to alter details like tax rates; you should also make sure that you can alter them easily and quickly, without any programming knowledge. If you look at your existing systems for a minute or two you may discover that they are much more flexible than you realised. For instance, perhaps some customers pay cash, some are invoiced, others pay on receipt of proforma invoices before goods are dispatched. Will your order processing/ invoicing/sales ledger package do that?

Will a payroll package cope equally well with hourly-, weekly-, monthly- paid, part-time employees, contractors, bonuses, commissions, saving schemes, pensions, sick pay, holiday pay, etc., etc.? Can you add your own words to a spelling checker? Can you set up your programs to run when you want or must you follow a daily or weekly or monthly cycle? Can you run independent systems for each project, each department or separate companies - and perhaps consolidate them later? Can you design your own formats for charts or graphs - or must you select from standard options? And some users might be concerned if they never get the chance of using the black pieces, or actually being the Red Baron, rather than always shooting him down!

When you have become familiar with a package, can you reduce the 'help level' so as to eliminate the more basic menus and instructions? If not, a package which is quite easy to learn may become tiresome to use in the long run.

GUIDELINE 6 : Will the Package be Easy to Use?

Is the 'user interface' easy to understand? Translated, that means will the average user be able to read, understand and act on the information presented on screen? Are menus, or other methods of making choices, clear? Are users likely to get 'stuck'? A similar question concerns the verbiage surrounding the system. Are the manuals, help screens and any other user documentation easy to read? Would they really help you to carry out some function which you did not already know how to do?

How does the package cope with errors? Does it protect the user from mistakes? Is it easy to 'crash' the system with incorrect data? Can you understand the error messages which may crop up? (They are often listed as an Appendix in the back of the manual.)

How much floppy swapping is needed in normal operation of the package? This is hard to assess when you see a package being demonstrated; on the one hand, you may not notice how much time is taken up by floppy swapping (the system may be installed on hard disk, or the salesperson may take your mind off it) - but on the other hand, there may be more floppy swapping than normal, in order to show you all aspects of the package during the demonstration. You must try to judge this, or talk if possible to unbiased users who have been using the package for some time. Hard disk users will not usually face this problem. Some of the worst forms of copy protection, though, which do not include a proper hard disk installation option, may force you to keep changing floppy disks, even though you have plenty of room on your hard disk.

Does the package have special requirements? For instance, many packages recommend the use of pre-printed stationery, which looks more professional in any event. Some programs are flexible enough, however, to give you an option to print headings: useful if you don't wish to use specially printed stationery - or if you run out. Another point on programs which print on special forms: do they include a printer line-up routine, or will you have to waste several pages of stationery and re-start the print run if the form is not perfectly lined up first time? Other programs have peculiar hardware or software requirements e.g. particular input/output devices or operating environments such as Microsoft's Windows. These may not rule out the package but may affect its ease of use and must obviously feature in your cost calculations.

Is the package copy-protected? It may be impossible to install it to a hard disk; it will almost certainly be impossible to copy it to a RAM disk. Either way, the package is harder to use than it should be. The worst kind can only be run by restarting or resetting your computer, often because they cannot run under DOS, let alone GEM, making it impossible to switch smoothly between applications. Forget about your convenient DOS menus or your neatly laid-out Desktop - to run these user-hostile programs you must give them exclusive rights over your PC. There is no effective remedy. However frustrating this might be, you are advised to stay well away from the illegal business of copying protected software (except when authorised for backup purposes) and of course never to buy pirate copies. The best policy is to avoid, where possible, using copy-protected software at all; there is usually an alternative of high quality.

Is the package 'integrated'? Many popular packages perform several functions; the classic Lotus 1-2-3 combines the functions of a simple database, a graphics program and a spreadsheet. This is a good example of integration, because you can speedily draw graphs or charts from the data in a spreadsheet; the data is readily available to all parts of the package. But don't take claims of 'integration' for granted. Many so-called integrated packages consist of separate modules which communicate between each other with difficulty, if at all. Look out for awkard 'export' and 'import' procedures, or programs bridging or sending batch files between modules; they are fiddly, time-consuming and error-prone. Some accounts packages are particularly clumsy in this respect.

For many PC users, integration is not a priority. Strangely enough, Lotus 1-2-3 exemplifies this, too; many people use it solely as a spreadsheet. For 'multi-function' packages, integration is usually a trade-off between power and convenience. If you want a really powerful database or graphics program, you are more likely to find it as a stand-alone program than as part of an integrated package.

 If you need an integrated package, make sure that the integration is automatic

GUIDELINE 7 : Try Before You Buy

Try to use the package yourself, rather than just sit and passively watch a demonstration. Any professional supplier is bound to rehearse demonstrations until they are almost perfect, inevitably highlighting the better features if not actually concealing others. Your dealer may justifiably refuse to let you borrow the package but see if you can sit down at their premises and find your way around the program. If you have to rely on a demonstration, take an active part and ask plenty of questions, including any you have jotted down beforehand. Many software vendors will send you a demonstration disk, particularly for more expensive packages. This may contain just a 'storyboard' presentation of the major features; better ones actually give you a cut-down version of the actual program e.g. a database which can take no more than twenty records. You can get a good feel for the package in this way, as long as you allow for the fact that you are not using realistic volumes of data.

GUIDELINE 8 : Talk to Existing Users

This is an excellent way of getting hard information about software, especially its weaknesses and how it performs in everyday use. Be very wary of a supplier who cannot put you in touch with one or two customers with at least a couple of months' experience of the package. Two further caveats: occasionally you will encounter users who feel obliged to justify every purchase they have made, including the wrong ones! More rarely, you might find yourself talking to a 'tame' customer, possibly taking a commission from the software vendor.

GUIDELINE 9 : Consider the Supplier as Well as the Package

However brilliant a program, it will contain bugs. It is therefore only as good as the support which the software company and/or the dealer will provide. In particular, what is their policy for updating the program and what resources do they provide to support it? Ask what is the current release level of the package and how frequent are new releases. What is the charge, if any, for upgrading to an enhanced version? Generally it is worth paying the nominal charge which is usually made to stay at the latest level. How rapidly are major and minor bugs fixed? In those cases, do you receive a free update?

Some packages may need modification when legislation changes. The classic example is a payroll package, which may need one or two updates every year just to cope with legal changes, let alone any bugs which may emerge! Does the supplier guarantee to issue updates whenever legally necessary?

It is always reassuring to deal with companies - and packages - with solid track records, but don't rule out new companies or products on that criterion alone. Bear in mind that hardly any PC software companies can yet boast of a ten-year track record. The availability, quality and cost of training and other support services such as consultancy and technical 'hotlines' should also be considered when choosing a software supplier. By the way, you might try out a 'hotline' number in advance, just to see if you can get through. I recently reached a very lukewarm software support line: making connection after about twenty redials, I was told that 'Our hotline only works on Thursday mornings'!

GUIDELINE 10 : Don't Be the First User

While new products can be outstanding, they can also be bug-ridden. Unless you have no choice, avoid the very first release of a software product. Whether or not it is a deliberate policy, some software companies effectively rely on early customers to carry out final testing for them!

GUIDELINE 11 : Don't Be the Last User

Ask the supplier frankly about product plans; it is very annoying to find that you have just bought an obsolete program. Make separate inquiries about the latest release level of the package you are considering. One or two dealers, sad to say, will sell you an out-of-date version just to clear old stocks. That is fair enough if they tell you about the latest release and offer a hefty discount on the earlier one, but buying the up-to-date version is always recommended.

GUIDELINE 12 : Don't Rely on Promises

Never buy software (or hardware) on the basis of a salesperson's promises of features, unless and until you have seen those features in action. The level of professionalism among micro salespeople is generally quite high (and probably improving) but, as in any industry, there are inevitable exceptions. Leaving aside the very rare cases of deliberate attempts to mislead, salespeople some-times simply do not know what their products can do. If for any reason you cannot see the features you need actually working, make your purchase conditional on them - and get something in writing.

GUIDELINE 13 : Don't Buy 'Vapourware'

'Vapourware' is the pejorative term used in the computer industry for products which, though announced, do not as yet exist. Clearly you should never buy such software (or hardware). Nor should you let such pre-announcements delay your decisions to buy other packages. Vapourware, when it materialises, is usually late and often disappointing.

GUIDELINE 14 : Consider Installation and Training

Many users forget to take into account the time and effort required for initial setup of the system, including the (often laborious) task of loading data into the necessary files; it always takes longer than you think. Just locating and loading the data for, say, a complete suite of accounts ledgers could take one person two weeks. Depending on that individual's seniority, the costs (salary plus overheads) of his or her time can even exceed the cost of the packages themselves.

Where training in the use of software may be needed, the cost and time involved should also be included in your calculations. Managers tend to concentrate on the training fees, the most obvious costs of training, while ignoring the opportunity cost of having key personnel away from work for several days: though hidden, this is often a higher cost. Whether you are self-employed or working for a large company, these factors still apply.

 Don't forget to budget for the direct and indirect costs of installation and training

Don't forget to schedule installation and training

GUIDELINE 15 : The Three 'U's

Finally, a quick test: if you ignore all the above details when choosing software, but instead just honestly answer the following three questions, you will not go too far wrong.

 Is the software really Useful?

Is the software really User-friendly?

Will you (or your colleagues) really Use it?

If you hesitate in giving a clear 'Yes' to any of these questions, don't spend too much money!

CHECKLISTS

If you want to make your selection a little more rigorous, you can of course use a checklist. The simplest is merely a list of the features you want from the package. When assessing a product, you put a tick beside each feature which it offers. Repeat the process with a separate column for each product under review and the column with the most ticks normally indicates the package best suited to your needs. Of course this is rather crude. The package with the greatest number of desired features might not have one of the most important features. This is simply remedied by splitting the features into two categories: essential and desirable. A checklist might then look something like this:

Product	A	B	C	
Essential:				
Feature 1	✓	✓	✓	
Feature 2	✓		✓	
Feature 3	✓	✓	✓	
Feature 4	✓	✓	✓	
Desirable:				
Feature 5		✓	✓	
Feature 6	✓	✓		
Feature 7	✓	✓	✓	

Any product, such as B in this example, which does not offer all the essential features, is then immediately eliminated. The decision in this case is between products A and C; the final choice probably depending on which of the 'nice-to-have' features you could most readily live without.

 A simple checklist showing essential and desirable features will help in most software selection tasks

If you find it difficult to resolve a 'tie', you might like to add a weighting to the features and a score to indicate how well each package performs in delivering each feature (weight x score = total). But don't get too fancy: it is easy to get carried away with elaborate scoring mechanisms, and to credit checklists with analytical powers which they do not possess.

Software Pricing

As we have seen, the supposedly 'upmarket' package, which enjoys a hefty advertising budget and usually a price to match, may not be the best buy. Don't rule them out, though: they are usually well supported and often fully justify their price. Most packages aimed at the Amstrad PC are more modestly priced, ranging from around £200-£300 downwards. Many programs seem to be bunched in the £50-£80 bracket, with a few available for as little as £30. There is an even lower price bracket, software which is, in theory, free.

Public Domain Software: 'Freeware' and 'Shareware'

So-called Freeware arose from PC enthusiasts who, several years ago, began forming themselves into Software Interest Groups (SIGs) who exchanged software freely amongst their members. This activity, boosted (in the US at least) by computer 'bulletin boards' and other forms of electronic mail, has now been extended to make Freeware available to all PC users. The groups distributing these programs in the UK, some of which levy a membership fee, make a nominal charge to cover the costs of disks, postage etc. Hundreds of PC programs are available; the user receives just a disk, including a text file called READ.ME, which describes how the program works. Copies can be made and given to friends.

Shareware is similar. Copying and sharing is encouraged although the author does retain copyright in this case. If you find a program useful then you are encouraged to send a donation to the author (a specific sum is often suggested). The incentive for the user to make such a payment is that registered contributors receive free upgrades of the program, extra features and, perhaps, a comprehensive manual. In addition, the person who supplied the original disk to the new subscriber may receive a small commission.

The benefit to the software developer is a cheap and often highly effective distribution channel. Some packages become so well established that they move into the mainstream software market to be sold by dealers like any other product. A good example is the word processing package PC Write; although an earlier release is still available as shareware, the program has now been repackaged by several suppliers who retail it just like any other package.

Numerous word processors, databases and spreadsheets are available as public domain software. There are also several languages, accounting packages, communications programs, graphics programs - and a host of utility programs for almost every conceivable purpose. Details of suppliers are given in the Appendix. The PC magazines sometimes conduct thorough reviews but in general there is a real shortage of hard information about the features, quality and reliability of these programs. For an outlay of perhaps £5 you might think you cannot go wrong. That is only partly true, for the costs of a serious software failure can be horrendous. By all means obtain freeware and shareware, but be cautious:

 Remember that the support you can expect is roughly proportional to software price. Near-zero price usually means zero support

Custom-built Software

What if you cannot seem to find the package/program you need? Early PC users faced a stark choice: write your own programs - or get someone to write them for you. The options now are wider:

1. Buy a standard package off-the-shelf and live with its limitations.
2. Find a package with greater flexibility for customisation to your needs. Customisation ranges from simple changes (e.g. to set up and configuration) to expensive program changes.
3. Use standard database and/or spreadsheet software packages.
4. Use a program generator or applications generator package.
5. Develop your own systems with conventional programming languages e.g. BASIC, C, COBOL, Pascal, etc.

Although there are some outstanding PC language products on the market e.g. Turbo Pascal, QuickBASIC, you are strongly advised against No. 5 unless you have (a) systems and programming experience and (b) a lot of time and patience. If you are still determined to do-it-yourself, choose No. 3 or 4. Developing reliable software is tricky, and remember the Law of Software Development:

All software development takes at least 50% longer than planned, even after allowing for the Law of Software Development!

Always get detailed, written estimates for software development; go for fixed price contracts when possible

Make sure that any software written or amended for you is well documented, in language which you can understand. Otherwise you may find yourself forced in future to use the services of the same individual or organisation, simply because nobody else can understand the internal details of your system! As suggested at the beginning of this chapter, the best advice for over 99% of PC users, who are considering developing their own systems, is: *don't!*

How to purchase

Having found a reasonable dealer, especially one who lets you try before you buy, then you might feel that it is only fair to buy your software where you evaluate it, even if the price does not quite match the cheapest mail order price you have seen. If, however, you have decided on the strength of a recommendation or a review, or even a software developer's demonstration at an exhibition, then it would not be unreasonable to go for the best mail order deal. Before you do, though, make sure you are happy about the supplier's upgrade policy (see Guideline 9 above). Ordering by credit card can give you some protection against buying a faulty piece of software; you may be able to claim a refund from the credit card company.

If you have any doubts about a package, you may be advised to order in writing, specifying exactly what you understand it to be capable of doing; better still, get the supplier to confirm the feature(s) to you in writing. This applies whether you are paying £500 or £50 for your software. Only when the price has come down to £5, and you are buying public domain software, should you be prepared to accept the element of 'pot luck'. Finally, having bought your software, to make sure you receive full details of upgrades and new products:

Don't forget to register as an authorised user, by completing and sending back the postcard which usually comes with the program

Chapter Ten
Getting Programs Running

We saw in Chapter 4 how to get any program running, whether you are running it from floppy or hard disk - but we assumed that it had been properly set up in the first place; this is not always as simple as the software supplier may claim. Let us review the main steps in preparing any program for rapid startup and day-to-day running. It is obviously important to know whether the program is going to be started up from the GEM Desktop or directly from DOS. Setup procedures for both cases are described below.

First of all, take backup copies of program disks; don't wait until you have installed the software: that might be too late

Put write-protect tabs on your program disks before copying them; that way you cannot overwrite them by mistake

Installation and Configuration

Most programs require installation. This process includes making sure that all the program files and associated files are in the right places, which in turn requires that the program 'knows' what disk drives, printers, memory, screens, etc. your system has attached. The system must also know what type of application it is dealing with: GEM or DOS, does the program need additional parameters in order to run properly, etc. Providing this type of information is usually called configuration. Read carefully the user manual for the particular package. It should tell you exactly how to install and/or configure the system; usually you will find a ready-to-run install procedure. This may well include an initial backup process - but check before you run it.

Some programs may need no installation procedures. This, however, is rare; in any event, most packages have to be told, for example, whether you have a hard disk or printer installed. If your manual does not tell you whether installation is needed and exactly how to go about it, then the dealer who supplied the software will advise you. In the absence of any installation program, or clear instructions as to the procedures involved, it may be best to get professional help to install the package. Some users prefer to try the package and see if the results look right; if the screen display or printed output seems wrong, then something has clearly been neglected! This approach is not recommended.

Setting Up DOS Programs - How NOT to do it

The long-winded way to run a DOS program goes something like this. Floppy users start up the system with the MS-DOS disk (1512 hard disk users select MS-DOS from the menu). Set the date and time. Issue any necessary DOS commands e.g. to change the default disk drive and/or directory, set up keyboard, screen or printer, etc. Set up RAM disk if required. Swap floppies to insert the relevant program disk. Type in the command(s) to start the program running. Choose the program option to setup/configure the screen display, printer drivers, etc. Possibly swap program disks again to load the main program(s). Type in appropriate commands. Insert data disk if required. Change the default disk for data storage. Load (or create) any required file and eventually .... start work!

The prime objective when installing/configuring software is to ensure that it works as you intend. But another vital objective is to save time; many of the above steps can be speeded up or eliminated. If you can save as little as one minute each time you start running a program which you use, perhaps, twice a day, you will end up with a free hour every month!

Users without the luxury of a hard disk will make major time savings by reducing floppy swapping to a minimum. In particular, the tiresome business of loading DOS (from your working copy of floppy disk 1) then loading your program disk can nearly always be speeded up by creating a special startup disk First create a system disk, by formatting a blank disk as shown in Chapter 4, but make it a system disk with the /S switch, thus: FORMAT B:/S ENTER.

This creates a 'bootable' disk i.e. one with which you can start (or restart with Ctrl-Alt-Del) your PC. Instead of containing *all* the MS-DOS files, it will just contain the command processor COMMAND.COM and two hidden MS-DOS system files. Second, copy on to this disk any other MS-DOS commands and system files you know you will need to use in order that the program will run as intended. These might include e.g. KEYBUK.EXE, MODE.EXE, MOUSE.COM, etc.

Third, copy on to this disk the necessary program files along with ancillary files which the program needs available. The manual should tell you which files you need; if all the files on the original program disk will fit on to your startup disk, then you might as well copy them all across. If you do not have enough room for the required files, check carefully what each one is for. It may be, for instance, that many of the files on the original program disk(s) are demonstration files or perhaps extra printer drivers which you won't need, unless you change printers. There may be a section of the package which you decide you do not need on-line at all times e.g. a year-end or a mail-merge option. However you arrange it, you should now have a disk which you can use to start your system and, on keying in the correct commands, to run your program.

Hard disk users are unlikely to have space problems; they can copy all the files from their original program disks into a directory especially set up for this particular application, probably creating another directory purely for data files. If the original software was 'copy-protected', the normal COPY command will not work to copy programs in this way; the package must be installed to the hard disk using a special program supplied. It may be necessary, with some of the nastier types of copy protection, to have the original floppy in a disk drive even though you are actually running from hard disk.

Startup can now be further automated with an AUTOEXEC.BAT file (see Chapter 8 for full details, and examples of the commands which such a file may contain). This file can do all the fiddling about with dates, times, default drives/directories, RAM disks, devices (screen, printer, etc.) as well as actually starting the program running for you - without your having to press a single key. It can do invaluable housekeeping chores like automatically taking backups, keeping logs, and so on. Remember to include on the startup disk the CONFIG.SYS file, specifying e.g. country, files and buffers.

Installation details

The installation procedure may require you to specify e.g. number and type of disk drives, storage, screen, printer etc. Much of the data which may be needed is available in Appendix IV of your main Amstrad manual. When specifying screen details for a PC1512 the best results are usually obtained by specifying 'colour' or 'RGB' monitor even if you actually have a monochrome model. If you have a PC1640 model you must set the the internal graphics adapter (IGA) switches at the back of your machine, according to the graphics output of the software. The manual should say what the program requires: e.g. Hercules compatible (monochrome) or one of various degrees of colour resolution.

If the installation program enquires about your mouse, reply that it is a Microsoft type (unless specifying Amstrad itself is an available option). For specifying your printer, take care to get the make and model number correct (quoting a similar model occasionally works, if yours isn't listed).

Printer drivers

Packages handle printer drivers in different ways. You may need a separate driver for each different typeface. For matrix-type printers, this may include one for draft and one for letter quality in each typeface you intend to use. One particular driver may be defined as the default, which is loaded and used unless you specify otherwise. Remember that just having the required printer driver sitting around on disk will achieve nothing unless it is actually installed and loaded for use! Some packages include command files for loading printer drivers; these commands can be included in batch files such as AUTOEXEC.BAT, thus saving you from remembering and typing in yet another command sequence!

Telling DOS where to look for command files

It is often important to tell DOS where to look for commands or programs which it needs. It will always look in the current directory of the default drive but it is not always possible or desirable to keep all such files there. The command: PATH C:\;A:\;B:\ tells DOS to search the current directories of drives C, A and B in order to find any command or program it needs.

This command may need expanding to include subdirectories. For example, an HD user might store all the MS-DOS external commands in one subdirectory (called MSDOS) and a variety of batch files (each used for starting up a different application) in another (called BATFILES). This user might include a command such as:

PATH C:\;C:\MSDOS;C:\BATFILES;A:\

in the AUTOEXEC.BAT file. The individual startup batch files would, of course, switch to the specific subdirectories for each applications program.

 Don't assume that DOS will know where to find programs or commands; make sure that an appropriate path statement has been executed. Remember that the PATH command does not change the current directory

Setting Up Programs to Run under GEM

Many of the steps suggested above in installing software and setting up a startup disk are equally applicable for programs which can be run from GEM. The main Amstrad PC manual gives an example describing all the files required to set up a GEM Paint disk. Similarly, for any other application, you will need all the relevant program and associated files available on (preferably a single) disk; the program's own installation procedure must be completed as usual. Equally, you will still save a good deal of time by putting all the normal housekeeping business into an AUTOEXEC.BAT file; otherwise, you will have to exit to DOS and issue all the necessary commands individually.

Of course, instead of starting applications programs automatically by putting the relevant command (or menu choice if you have several applications available) into a batch file, you can just start them from the GEM Desktop. The last command in your batch file, the command 'GEM', would start GEM itself. When the Desktop is displayed, you would start the application by double-clicking on the relevant GEM icon rather than by typing in a command.

Configuring applications under GEM

Before you can click away and run your programs, however, you must first tell GEM about each one by using the 'Configure Application' option, which works as follows.
1. Click once on the icon for the program you want to configure (it must be of filetype .COM, .EXE, .APP or .BAT)
2. Pull down the 'Options' menu
3. Click once on the 'Configure Application' option
You then enter the relevant details in the Dialog Box which appears. If the program is specifically designed as a GEM application i.e. using GEM menus, icons, windows, etc. then click on GEM as the 'Application Type'.

If, however, it is essentially a DOS-based application, but one which you would find it convenient to run from the GEM Desktop, you must give GEM answers to two more questions. Firstly, does the DOS application require 'parameters'? That is to say, if you were starting the program (let's call it Supaprog) from the DOS prompt (A> etc.) would it require extra information to start it running e.g. SUPAPROG DATA8805 /A ? If so, click on 'DOS - takes parameters'. But if you would start it by just keying in the program name alone, just click the mouse button with the pointer on 'DOS'.

Secondly, does the application require all your available memory? When GEM is managing your computing, it makes life easier if GEM itself can stay in memory while you run your applications program; that way, as soon as you leave your program, your GEM desktop will appear again, enabling you rapidly to choose your next application. Some programs, unfortunately, are too hungry for memory: they insist on kicking GEM out so that they can use all your available RAM. When you exit from the latter type of program, you find yourself back at the DOS prompt. You then have to take the trouble to reload GEM and your desktop.

If your manual is unclear as to whether the program will co-exist with GEM, try it. Answer 'No' to the question 'Needs Full Memory?' and click on 'Install'. If the program runs out of memory (it may tell you, or it may just grind to a halt) you will have to re-configure the application, this time answering 'Yes' to the question 'Needs Full Memory'.

Two other features of the configuration process demonstrate the potential ease of use which GEM can provide. You can specify the filetype(s) of documents used by your application and then choose appropriate icons, for both program and documents. Suppose for example, you were installing a word processing package called SupaWord, which kept its documents in files with names like REPORT21.DOC. You could first type DOC where the Configure Application Dialog Box says 'Document Types', then scroll through the icon choices (by moving the 'Icon Type' scroll bar) until you find the suitable word processing icons. Click on 'Install' and these icons are now displayed on any SupaWord files on your Desktop.

So what? Well, in the first place you have an instant visual check on which files (program or documents) belong to SupaWord, which may save you some searching - it is certainly better than peering at long directory listings. What is more you can now double-click on a *document* (as an alternative to clicking on the program, selecting a 'Load Document' or 'Edit Document' option, then typing in the document name). Because GEM now knows which program is associated with this document, it will run the program and load the required document in one operation. It only saves a few seconds, but you save those few seconds every time you load a document.

 Don't forget to save your Desktop after any program configuration or re-configuration, otherwise all the details will be lost

Some users find the mouse itself hard to get used to. Make sure you have a smooth flat surface for it to roll around otherwise the pointer movement may be jerky and difficult to control. You can adjust both the scale of mouse movement (this is an option within the NVR program, which we used in Chapter 8 to alter the size of the RAM disk) as well as the speed of the double click (choose 'Set Preferences' from the 'Options' menu). One further thought:

 Pressing Enter to choose the default option (usually highlighted) on a GEM Dialog Box is often quicker than re-positioning and clicking the mouse

RUNNING BASIC 2 PROGRAMS

BASIC 2, supplied by Locomotive Software Ltd., is an interesting version of the BASIC language. Its major benefits are:

1. It is easy to learn.
2. It is relatively fast in execution compared to other BASICs.
3. It includes a number of features which can assist the programmer in writing well-structured programs.
4. It uses the GEM-style facilities of windows, menus and mouse-driven pointer. This is particularly useful, for example, if you want to develop and test your own programs - but it does mean that floppy disk users must first startup GEM, then load their GEM Desktop, then BASIC 2, which some users may find tedious. (See below for a quicker floppy route to BASIC 2.)
5. It has some very neat graphics capabilities.

The only serious drawback is its lack of compatibility with the version(s) of BASIC supplied by Microsoft, which is as near as the PC world has come to a standard language. But this does not mean that Locomotive BASIC 2 is anything less than a good implementation of the language, with clever and powerful features of which they (Locomotive) can be proud. Indeed, if you decide to write your own programs you may decide that BASIC 2 will do nicely.

BASIC 2 is started from the GEM Desktop by double-clicking with the mouse on the BASIC2 icon in order to open the BASIC2 folder. Now double-click on the BASIC2.APP icon and the typical BASIC 2 screen is displayed, with the three main windows:

The *Dialogue* (Locomotive use the English spelling) window shows commands which you key in, such as Run to start a program running, or Edit to change an existing program (or create a new one). It also displays messages from BASIC 2 to you.

The *Edit* window is where you actually work on the current program, to correct error or make enhancements. Type EDIT ENTER in the Dialogue window and the cursor jumps to the Edit window.

The *Results-1* window shows the output from the program when it is run. All the output can be shown in the Results-1 window, but the extra output window (Results-2) can be used, for instance, if you want a program to keep graphics output separate from text output.

An existing BASIC 2 program is loaded and run as follows:

1. Pull down the File menu.
2. Click on the Load option; the Item Selector Dialog box will appear, showing you all the available BASIC 2 programs (their filetype is .BAS). You may need to use the scroll bars if all the programs available cannot be displayed at once.
3. Double-click on the program you want (alternatively, click once to select it, then click on OK).
4. Type Run RETURN in the Dialogue window (alternatively, select Run or press F9, having pulled down the Program Menu).

A quicker way to run a BASIC 2 program from the GEM Desktop (having opened the BASIC2 folder) is simply to double-click on the program icon itself, rather than selecting BASIC2.APP. Because GEM knows that files of filetype .BAS should be BASIC 2 programs, it will load BASIC 2, then run the chosen program in one go.

BASIC 2 startup disks

Dual-floppy disk users who wish to avoid going via the Desktop can set up a startup disk and a BASIC 2 disk along the following lines (there are many ways of setting this up). Startup disk contains, say:

Root directory contains:	GEMSYS directory contains:
COMMAND.COM	OUTPUT.APP
NVRPATCH.EXE	DEFAULT.OPT
RPED.EXE	OUTPUT.RSC
CONFIG.SYS	METAFIL6.SYS
RAMDRIVE.SYS	GEMVDI.EXE
MOUSE.COM	AMSTRAD.SYS
KEYBUK.EXE	ASSIGN.SYS
AUTOEXEC.BAT	AMSLSS10.FNT
	AMSLSS14.FNT
AUTOEXEC.BAT could contain:	AMSLSS18.FNT
ECHO OFF	AMSLTR10.FNT
PROMPT PG	AMSLTR14.FNT
KEYBUK	AMSLTR18.FNT
MOUSE	
NVRPATCH	GEMBOOT directory contains:
CD\GEMSYS	SNAPSHOT.ACC
PATH B:\BASIC2	SNAPSHOT.RSC
GEMVDI BASIC2	CALCLOCK.ACC
	GEM.EXE
	GEM.RSC

The BASIC 2 disk would hold any programs and the BASIC2 language itself (APP and RSC files). The eventual benefit of all that copying is that you would simply place the startup disk in drive A, the BASIC 2 disk in drive B, and reset your PC. After a short delay, BASIC 2 is up and running.

Further points to note about BASIC 2

PC1512 users who have not upgraded their RAM to 640K may find space a bit tight, especially if they want to use all the desktop accessories and/or a RAM disk. As one BASIC 2 program cannot call another (i.e. you cannot execute a second program from within the first one) this may limit the complexity of your programs.

At the time of writing, subroutines could be used in BASIC 2 only by means of the GOSUB..... RETURN.... statements. Readers with programming experience will know that this is much less satisfactory than a DO or CALL or PERFORM statement, used in conjunction with predefined procedures. However, Locomotive assure me that a statement, enabling proper procedures to be used, will feature in a forthcoming release.

Any complex piece of software inevitably contains bugs. BASIC 2 is no exception; a small number of bugs have been identified and corrected. Space does not permit publication here of 'fixes' for these minor problems; in any case, it is fiddly, time-consuming and risky to attempt to patch up software by keying in corrections to the interpreter. Far better simply to send off your original disk to Locomotive with £5.95; they will send you the latest version. Some of the user groups may be able to give you a free upgrade.

The latest release at the time of writing was version 1.21 - but that will almost certainly be out of date when you read this. If you do not know which version you have, select the 'About BASIC 2' option from the BASIC 2 menu.

Manuals

Anyone intending to write serious programs using BASIC 2 must obtain, at the very least, the full BASIC 2 manual (available from Amsoft). They will probably also benefit from the complete Technical Reference manual from Locomotive Software Ltd.

Appendix
PC Software Survey

The following pages list, with a few words of description, some of the leading packages available which will run on the Amstrad PC 1512 or 1640 (some hardware add-ons are also included). Space does not permit an exhaustive survey; the categories chosen inevitably overlap. Programming language interpreters and compilers have been omitted. No prices are quoted as they are so volatile, but suppliers names and telephone numbers are given where known.

1. Data Management: Basic File Managers

CARDBOX (very easy-to-use yet flexible, low-cost, 'card index' manager, Caxton 01 379 6502)
CONDOR (reasonably friendly file manager, more power than Cardbox, inexpensive, Caxton 01 379 6502)
DATAEASE (clever, 'screen-painting' method quite easy to learn, Sapphire 01 554 0582)
FLYING START (low-cost file manager with indexing, easy searching, custom reports, Mitre 01 283 4646)
INFOMASTER (low-cost menu-driven database, quite easy to learn, can exchange data with other packages, Amstrad 0277 230222)
KEEPIT (simple database, links with other IT modules, Hoskyns 01 434 2171)
RAPIDFILE (flexible, fast data entry/retrieval/reporting, Ashton-Tate 0628 33123)
REFLEX (easy to learn 'flat-file' data manager with clever ways of examining/ analysing data, Borland 01 258 3797)
RETRIEVE (flat file manager, quite easy-to-use enquiry methods, could be used for mailmerging, Sagesoft 091 284 7077)
SUPERFILE (unusual record structure, quite powerful but not cheap, Southdata 01 727 7564)

2. Data Management: Relational Databases

dBASE II, III, III+, IV (family of powerful, best-selling products with built-in language, II is not for novices, III and IV have friendlier 'ASSIST' modes and huge capacity/multiple file handling, III+ is network version, Ashton-Tate 0628 33123)
PARADOX (outstanding program, combines great power with ease of use and learning, Borland 01 258 3797)

POWERBASE (well-designed 'intermediate' database, custom forms/menus/reports but no built-in programming language, Namic 0582 28463)
RBASE (powerful, quite easy-to-use, links well to 1-2-3 etc., built-in programming language, Microsoft 0734 500741)
SUPERBASE PERSONAL 1512 (mouse-driven, some nice touches, multiple files but simpler than dBASE-type products, Precision Software 01 330 7166)
TAS PLUS (very reasonably-priced, easy-to-learn yet powerful program, built-in language for experienced users, Megatech 01 874 6511)

3. Integrated Packages

ABILITY (remarkable power for the low price, easy-to-learn, well integrated, word processing, spreadsheet, graphics, database, communications, Ability Plus has even more features, including more powerful database, Migent 01 499 4752)
FIRST CHOICE (word processing, spreadsheet, file manager and communications, runs only one task at a time, easy to switch tasks but must run transfer routines to pass data between applications, Software Publishing 01 839 2849)
FRAMEWORK II (database, word processing, spreadsheet, graphics, robust package, requires at least two floppies, Ashton-Tate 0628 33123)
LOTUS 1-2-3 (strictly an integrated package, but database is negligible, graphics OK, but its strength is as a spreadsheet, see below, Lotus 0753 840281)
OPEN ACCESS (one of the most effective integrated packages, six modules linking well, including good graphics, SPI 0735 74081)
PC-FOUR (good value package, easy word processor, spreadsheet, database, and graphics, but transfer between modules could be easier, Psion 01 723 9408)
SMART (spreadsheet, word processor and data manager, all three are well-designed and the integration is well achieved, Paradigm 01 228 5008)
SYMPHONY (not as successful as its stable-mate 1-2-3, RAM-hungry, the spreadsheet is the major module, Lotus 0753 840281)

4. Accounting and Finance

ACCOUNT ABILITY (more accounts features than Ability (see under integrated packages above), Migent
BOS (comprehensive, multi-user packages for medium/larger companies, hard disk vital, BOS 01 831 8811)
COMPACT (Daybook version for smaller businesses, Accounts version includes sales/purchase ledgers, stock control and invoicing, Compact 0306 887373)
DAC-EASY (well-integrated, low-cost package converted from US original, takes some getting used to, but powerful features including forecasting and custom reports, Technology Software 0483 898140)
DESKTOP ACCOUNTANT (invoicing, sales & purchase ledgers, up to 65,000 accounts, Caxton 01 379 6502)
FREEWAY (sales, purchase and payroll, Freeway are 'giving away' the package at nominal cost in order to get it established, Freeway 0942 826329)
MICROLEDGER (low-cost bookkeeping: sales, purchase, nominal ledger plus petty cash, all fits on one floppy, Textstore 01 891 1244)
MICROFACTS (mid-priced suite of programs, quite easy to use, also Microfacts+ network version, Microfacts 0234 218191)

PEGASUS (one of the market leaders at the mid/top end of PC accounting, all the usual modules: sales, purchase, nominal ledgers, payroll, stock control, order processing plus job costing and (unusually) bill of materials, well written and well integrated, Pegasus 0536 522822)

POWERSYSTEMS (range of higher-priced, feature-packed programs for professional accountants, facilitate setting up more complex accounts structures and reports, Omicron 01 938 2244)

SAGE (Bookkeeper, Payroll, Accountant, Accountant+, Financial Controller; reasonably priced, straightforward packages, Financial Controller is well-integrated but payroll is separate, programs have modest appetite for disk storage (Accountant fits a set of ledger programs on one floppy), have sold well to small/medium businesses, Sage 091 284 7077)

SKYMASTER (higher-priced, sales/purchase/nominal/payroll/stock control/order processing/job costing, multi-user version available, Sky 0527 36299)

SNIP (low-cost integrated package, originally priced much higher, HAT 0963 24551)

SUNACCOUNT (higher-priced, multi-user, large company, accountants' programs, Systems Union 01 354 3131)

TAXSOFT (specialist tax programs, versions available for individuals and companies, Quantec 01 228 7507)

TETRAPLAN (powerful, multi-user, programs, for larger users, Tetra 0494 450291)

5. Spreadsheets, Planning and Statistics

EXECUSTAT (heavily graphics-oriented, perhaps easier to use than Statgraphics, more a business manager's than a statistician's tool, can transfer data to/from e.g. 1-2-3 and dBASE, Mercia 021 359 5096)

IN CONTROL! (very low-cost project management package, critical path analysis, Gantt charts etc., excellent value, many features of its more expensive parent Pertmaster, Abtex 0274 734838)

K SPREAD 2 (one of the few programs to use GEM and the mouse, features include multiple windows, logical operations and sideways printing, Kuma 0735 74335)

LOTUS 1-2-3 (the accepted standard PC spreadsheet, now so well established that a host of 'templates': ready-designed sheets for standard applications and other add-ons are now available to enhance the package, not cheap but very robust and well-supported, Lotus 0753 840281)

OXSTAT (spreadsheet-based program with unusually sophisticated statistical routines built in, Wight 01 858 2699)

PC PLANNER (low-cost, competent spreadsheet, 1-2-3 compatible, decent well-integrated graphics, Sagesoft 091 284 7077)

SCRATCHPAD PLUS (inexpensive spreadsheet, all usual features,plus 'multiple windows' and a useful virtual memory feature for large sheets i.e. automatically starts using disk when RAM is full, Caxton 01 379 6502)

STATGRAPHICS (all the major statistical routines plus excellent integrated graphics (1640 screen display preferable), Cocking and Drury 01 493 6172)

SUPERCALC 3.21 (low-cost version of one the worldwide spreadsheet leaders, includes useful graphics features, accepts data from other packages, Amstrad 0277 230222)

SWIFT (very inexpensive, easier to use than most spreadsheets, limited graphics but good macro facility, Metamorphosis 0734 303078)

6. Graphics and Design

AUTOSKETCH (low-cost CAD package, from same company as Autocad, Autodesk 01 928 7868)
FREELANCE PLUS (flexible drawing package, ideally suited for charts for presentation purposes, accepts data from 1-2-3 and Symphony, Lotus 0753 840281)
GEM DRAW (easy to learn if you have tried GEM Paint, works with greater precision than its pixel-oriented cousin, Digital Research 0635 35304)
GEM GRAPH (pie/bar charts and line graphs, can take data from 1-2-3, dBASE etc., images can be manipulated with GEM Draw, Digital Research 0635 35304)
K GRAPH 2 (GEM-based charts and graphs package, Kuma 07357 4335)
TURBOCAD (powerful CAD packages available in low-cost and full versions, Pink Software 01 267 4499)
VCN CONCORDE (intended to produce business presentation graphics, includes library of symbols and images, accepts data from many packages, P & P 0706 217444)

7. Word Processing and Mailing

1ST WORD PLUS (inexpensive, WYSIWYG (what-you-see-is-what-you-get) program which makes full use of the GEM interface and the mouse, on-line spelling checker, pull-down menus, mail-merge, Electric Software 0480 66433)
BONNIE BLUE (powerful but inexpensive single-disk program, includes indexes, wordcount, macros, although no spelling checker, Paperlogic 01 935 0480)
GEM WRITE (obviously uses GEM and mouse, can incorporate GEM Paint images, documents limited to RAM, Digital Research 0635 35304)
MANUSCRIPT (WYSIWYG technical authors' package, includes graphics facilities, special symbol sets, Lotus 0753 840281
PC-WRITE (competent package, spelling checker can run as you type, includes a mail-merge, Sage 091 284 7077, earlier versions available as public domain software)
TELEWRITER II (word processing with extensive communications facilities bundled in, price includes BT Gold and Easylink subscription, Bristol Software Factory 0272 735022)
VOLKSWRITER DELUXE (very low-cost but full-featured program, typing tutor thrown in, Lifetree 0494 772422)
VUWRITER (another low-cost program with some good features e.g. italics, European characters, often found only in pricier products, Vuman 061 226 8311)
WORD (top quality package, with advanced features, multiple typefaces etc., almost becoming a desktop publishing program, Microsoft 0734 500741)
WORD JUNIOR (cut-down version of the flagship Word product, well suited for keen mouse users, quick and easy to use, includes glossaries, footnotes and an Undelete - every word processor should feature this! Microsoft 0734 500741)
WORDPERFECT (outstanding product available in very presentable 'junior' version, SSI 0932 231164)

WORDSTAR 1512/1640 (despite some condescending reviews, easier to learn than many packages (including the original WordStar!) and a lot of features (including a good mailmerge option and spelling checker) for the price, quite heavy floppy swapping if no hard disk, Micropro but sold by Amstrad 0277 230222)

8. Desktop Publishing (DTP)

DESKTOP PUBLISHER'S GRAPHICS   (moderate price, fairly flexible, can be integrated with Pagemaker or Ventura, Eldoncray 0202 293407)
FLEET STREET EDITOR   (also modestly priced, reasonable graphics and text features, OK for newsletter production, Mirrorsoft 01 377 4644)
FONTASY (budget DTP program, Ctrl Alt Deli 0908 662759)
PAGEMAKER (superb program, the originator of all DTP packages, will accept text and graphics from numerous programs, elegant mouse-driven interface, requires Windows (equivalent to GEM), will run on a hard disk Amstrad, but slowly: really needs a 286 co-processor, Aldus 031 336 1727)
VENTURA (runs OK on hard disk Amstrad, uses mouse and GEM, early versions had a few bugs, good 'style sheet' features, Xitan 0703 871211)

9. Communications and Networks

AMNET (low-cost LAN (local area network) for Amstrad PCs, Real Time Developments 0252 546213)
BREAKOUT (a complete hardware/software package including a choice of internal or external modems, from PC Communications 0438 310145)
CHIT-CHAT (versatile package, access to Telecom Gold, Microlink, Easylink, also Viewdata (Prestel etc.), telex, can edit messages off-line, send timed messages automatically, Sagesoft 091 284 7077)
FLOPPYNET (save enormous time and trouble: copy your file(s) on to a floppy, walk to neighbouring office, put it in colleague's PC, load it up: you now have the lowest-cost easiest-to-use local network possible! Seriously, don't install a LAN unless you are confident of major benefits)
GEM COMM (links with other GEM modules to give quite a neatly integrated communications system, Digital Research 0635 35304)
PROCOMM (a shareware communications package, 0895 51978)

10. Games and Entertainment

ALEX HIGGINS SNOOKER   (Amstrad 0277 230???)
BALANCE OF POWER   (complex, intriguing Superpower simulation, Mirrorsoft 01 377 4644)
CYRUS II CHESS   (well-reviewed, has won micro chess tournaments, good display, Amstrad 0277 230222)
FLIGHT SIMULATOR   (a classic, runs well on 1512/1640, realistic simulation of flying a Cessna, Microsoft 0734 500741)
GATO (good WWII submarine simulation, Mirrorsoft 01 377 4644)
HITCHHIKERS' GUIDE TO THE GALAXY   (the game of the TV series of the radio program of the book, Infocom 01 431 1101)

HOBBIT (based on the Tolkein classic, huge seller on humbler computers, now on the PC, Melbourne House 01 377 8411)
MEAN 18 GOLF (Amstrad 0277 230222)
PITSTOP II (Amstrad 0277 230222)
PSION CHESS (outstanding program, 3-d graphics, remarkable playing ability, Psion 01 723 9408)
SILENT SERVICE (less cerebral sub. simulation than GATO, MicroProse 0666 54326)
SPECULATOR (fairly true-to-life, though not as rapid, simulation of futures trading, Xitan 0703 871211)
STARGLIDER (fast 3-D space shoot 'em up, Rainbird 01 240 8838)
SUMMER GAMES (and WINTER GAMES for that matter, Amstrad 0277 230222)
TRADER (more frenetic, if slightly less accurate, trading simulation, Greenco 0676 33395)
TRIVIAL PURSUIT (over 3000 stupid questions, Domark 01 947 5624)
WALL STREET (realistic stock market simulation, Xitan 0703 871211)
ZORK TRILOGY (supposedly addictive adventures, Infocom 01 431 1101)

11. Miscellaneous Software

AMSFIX (if you really cannot wait for your floppy disk lights to go out, this little program cuts down the delay! S & S 02403 4201)
BRAINSTORM ('ideas processor', inexpensive and useful program for organising thoughts, plans etc. into a logical structure, easy to learn and use, Caxton 01 379 6502)
CRUISE CONTROL (speeds up the cursor when moving around giant spreadsheets; sounds silly, but heavy spreadsheet users swear by it, Softsel 01 568 8866)
DESK-SET (memory resident utility, 'desktop organiser' pops up when needed, includes calendar, calculator, alarm clock, simple editor, telephone dialler, plus access to DOS without leaving your application, Sage 091 284 7077)
DSBACKUP (fast hard disk backup utility, Ctrl-Alt-Deli 0908 662759)
FASTBACK (even faster hard disk backup program, 10 MB in 10 minutes, Riva 04862 71001)
HAL ('natural language' 'front-end' for Lotus 1-2-3, fascinating product but some way to go before you can really talk to your spreadsheet the way you do to your accountant, Lotus 0753 840281)
MACE+ UTILITIES (good utility package rivalling Norton, P & P 01 677 7631)
MENUGEN (creates menu programs to protect the user from DOS, Microft 01 948 8255)
NORTON UTILITIES (best-selling package, may help to diagnose problems and retrieve lost data, P & P 01 677 7631)
PC AUTOMATOR (learns instruction sequences in a similar way to keyboard enhancers, more experienced users could develop an entire system with this package, Direct Technology 01 847 1666)
PORTEX (attempt to make 'organiser' software more practical, including e.g. printouts of diary/address book pages on to special sheets for Filofax-style portable binder, Showerings 01 922 8821)

PROKEY (one of the original 'keyboard enhancers' enabling you to teach your PC any sequence of keystrokes, which can then be recalled at the touch of a single key of your choice, P & P 01 677 7631)
SIDEKICK (world's best-selling desktop organiser, similar features to Deskset, Borland 01 258 3787)
SMARTKEY (another keyboard enhancer, Caxton 01 379 6502)
SMARTNOTES (RAM resident program which pops up when you want to annotate, say, an entry in a spreadsheet or database "Where did that figure come from?", Tekware 0483 898140)
SUPERKEY (a best-selling keyboard enhancer, Borland 01 258 3787)
THINKTANK (ideas processor, similar to Brainstorm, P & P 0706 217744)
TLO PLUS (applications generator i.e. program that writes programs, updated and debugged version of one of the first such generators, remarkable package, DJ 'AI' Systems 04605 4117)
TOUCH 'N' GO (simple, effective keyboard and touchtyping tutorial program, Caxton 01 379 6502)
TURBO LIGHTNING (RAM-resident spell-checker and thesaurus, potentially useful product but US spelling only so far, Borland 01 258 3787)

12. Public Domain Software and User Groups

1512 INDEPENDENT USER GROUP   0959 24955
BIG SOFTY 051 228 3844
COMPULINK USER GROUP   0483 573337
FREEWAY 0942 826329
IBM PC USER GROUP   01 232 2277
ISD (PD software) 021378 2229
OFFICIAL AMSTRAD PROFESSIONAL USERS CLUB   091 5673395
PD SIG 0895 51978
SELTEC (PD software) 0344 863020
SHAREWARE MARKETING   0732 358125

13. Hardware Add-Ons

RAM UPGRADE (for 1512 users. To bring your 1512 up to the (DOS 3.2) maximum of 640K (standard on the PC1640) you need 18 64K DRAM chips. Most dealers will supply and fit them, or you can DIY at your own risk. User groups will also sell you chip sets, or try Dataflex (01 543 6417) who package them with instructions for Amstrad users)
MODEMS (essential for all PC communications. Major suppliers include Dowty (0635 33009), Miracle (0473 216141) Pace (0274 488211) and Tandata (06845 68421). An internal card modem is available from Amstrad 0277 230222)
HARD DISKS (check that disks-on-a-card will fit under the Amstrad cover; some overhang two of your precious expansion slots. The Hardcard 10 from CMA (04867 4555) works fine, the Seagate from Golden Gate (0628 783631) is inexpensive, Qubie (01 871 2855) offer a choice of front-mounted or card-mounted 20 megabyte disks.
BERNOUILLI BOX (rigid removable cartridge disk drives, available in 10 and 20 MB sizes, making backup and security much easier, Iomega 01 903 2418)
TAPE STREAMERS (fairly convenient for HDbackups, Cristie 045382 3611)